The Awesome Book of DINOSAURS!

The Awesome Book of DINOSAURS!

by
Clizia Gussoni

Illustrated by
Luke McDonnell

RUNNING PRESS
KIDS
PHILADELPHIA·LONDON

Italian born and trained, **Clizia Gussoni** is co-founder and Creative Director of Gussoni-Yoe Studio, Inc., an innovative design firm housed in a mountaintop castle overlooking the Hudson River. Her clients are among the top names in corporate America: Disney, Warner Bros., Cartoon Network, MTV, Nickelodeon, Mattel, and Microsoft, to name but a few.

Clizia specializes in innovative design and creations and has garnered several awards in recognition of her accomplishments, including a Mobius and two Addys. She has been featured in various publications including *The New York Times, Li©ense! Magazine,* and *The Women's Business Journal.*

Library of Congress Control Number: 2005903192

ISBN-13: 978-0-7624-2643-0
ISBN-10: 0-7624-2643-8

This book may be ordered by mail from the publisher.
Please include $2.50 for postage and handling.
But try your bookstore first!

Published by Running Press Kids, an imprint of
Running Press Book Publishers
125 South Twenty-Second Street
Philadelphia, Pennsylvania 19103-4399

Visit us on the web!
www.runningpress.com

T. rex-sized THANK YOUs to the following people who, with their **creativity, patience,** and **dedication** have made this book possible: Jon Anderson, Craig Yoe, the great illustrator Luke McDonnell, Jayne Antipow, Rosalie Lent, Joy Court, Kris Reinhold, Amanda Bonavita, Mike Croswell, Mike Hill, Mike Marro, Mom and Dad, and Leonardo Salgado.
—*Clizia Gussoni*

Thanks to all the **dinosaurs** who posed for these pictures!
—*Luke McDonnell*

If you like dinosaurs as I do, you would love to be able to go back to the Age of Dinosaurs. That's when imposing beasts like T. rex ruled the earth and smaller plunderers like Velociraptor hunted for prey.

It was a time when being around without some form of defense was a risky business. But dinosaurs were smart. Some of them bore sturdy protective shields that were impossible to pierce, preceding the armor of the Middle Age knights by 65 million years (take or leave a few centuries). Others were huge or had enormous horns, claws, beaks, or neck frills. And if all else failed, some could run very fast.

I wrote this book so I can go back to the Age of Dinosaurs every time I flip through its pages. It's not as exciting as being there in person, finding myself surrounded by strange plants, avoiding running into an Allosaurus, or ending up under an Apatosaurus' foot. But at least it's not half as dangerous!

IN THIS **AWESOME BOOK,** YOU'LL FIND MANY **DINOSAUR DESCRIPTIONS.** THE **DIMENSIONS** FOR EACH **DINOSAUR** (HEIGHT, WEIGHT, AND LENGTH) ARE **APPROXIMATE** AND, IN SOME CASES, NOT AVAILABLE. IN BETWEEN THIS INFORMATION, THERE ARE **FACTS** ABOUT WHERE DINOSAURS **LIVED,** WHAT THEY **ATE,** WHO **DISCOVERED** THEM, AND **MORE!**

FOR DIFFICULT TERMS, CHECK OUT THE **GLOSSARY** AT THE END OF THE BOOK.

GLOSSARY

WHAT IS A DINOSAUR?

IN 1842, **SIR RICHARD OWEN** IDENTIFIED A GROUP OF **UNKNOWN PREHISTORIC ANIMALS** HE CALLED **"DINOSAURS."**

DINOSAUR MEANS **"TERRIBLE LIZARD."**

WE NOW KNOW THAT NOT ALL **DINOSAURS** WERE **TERRIBLE,** AND NONE WERE **LIZARDS.**

THE MAIN **CHARACTERISTIC** OF **DINOSAURS** WAS THEIR **UPRIGHT POSTURE,** ENABLING SOME DINOSAURS TO MOVE **SWIFTLY,** AND OTHERS TO GROW **MASSIVE.** DINOSAURS WERE THE **BIGGEST ANIMALS EVER** TO WALK ON **LAND.**

In the squat posture, typical in crocodiles, the legs are attached to the sides of the body. The animal crawls, swinging its body from side to side when walking.

In the dinosaur upright posture, the legs are attached under the body.

DINOSAURS WERE **REPTILES**. THEY HAD **SCALY SKIN** AND LAID **EGGS**. UNLIKE MANY REPTILES, DINOSAURS DIDN'T **SWIM** OR **FLY**.

Pterodactylus was a flying reptile, but it wasn't a dinosaur.

Ichthyosaurus was a marine reptile, but it wasn't a dinosaur either.

DINOSAURS EVOLVED FROM **THEOCODONTS,** ANCIENT REPTILES, DURING THE **TRIASSIC PERIOD.** THE FIRST DINOSAURS WERE **SMALL CARNIVOROUS BIPEDS.** THEY SOON TOOK OVER THE **EARTH** BY DIVERSIFYING. DINOSAURS EVOLVED INTO **MANY SPECIES,** WITH DIFFERENT **CHARACTERISTICS** AND **DIETS.**

Eoraptor is the oldest known dinosaur.

NAMING DINOSAURS

Tyrannosaurus rex

DINOSAURS' NAMES ARE COMPOSED OF **TWO** WORDS. THE **FIRST ONE** IS THE **GENUS NAME** AND IS ALWAYS **CAPITALIZED**. THE **SECOND ONE** IS THE **SPECIES NAME** AND IS ALWAYS **LOWER CASE**. THE SPECIES NAME IS SELDOM USED IN THIS BOOK.

THE **GENUS NAME** GENERALLY DESCRIBES A DINOSAUR'S **MAIN CHARACTERISTIC**. FOR EXAMPLE, **TYRANNOSAURUS** MEANS **TYRANT LIZARD**, A PERFECT NAME FOR SUCH A **SAVAGE ANIMAL**.

SOMETIMES THE **GENUS NAME** DESCRIBES THE **LOCATION** WHERE THE DINOSAUR WAS **DISCOVERED**. FOR EXAMPLE **EDMONTOSAURUS** WAS FOUND IN **EDMONTON, CANADA**.

FINALLY, A **GENUS NAME** CAN **HONOR A PALEONTOLOGIST'S WORK**. FOR EXAMPLE, **LAMBEOSAURUS** WAS NAMED BY **WILLIAM PARKS** TO HONOR FELLOW PALEONTOLOGIST **LAWRENCE LAMBE**.

Footnote: Scientists use Latin or Greek words to come up with new names. These languages are international and scientists from around the globe understand them.

SAURISCHIAN DINOSAURS

HARRY SEELEY WAS AN **ENGLISH SCIENTIST** WHO STUDIED MANY **FOSSILS.** IN **1887,** HE NOTICED THAT **ALL DINOSAURS** CAN BE DIVIDED INTO **TWO MAIN GROUPS.**

DEPENDING ON THE **SHAPE** OF THEIR **HIP BONE,** HE CALLED THEM **SAURISCHIAN,** WHICH MEANS "**LIZARD-HIPPED,**" AND **ORNITHISCHIAN,** WHICH MEANS "**BIRD-HIPPED.**"

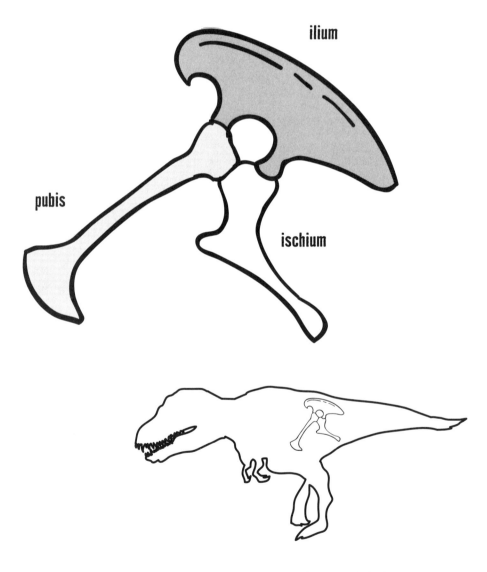

ilium

pubis

ischium

A DINOSAUR **HIP BONE** WAS MADE OF THREE BONES; **ILIUM, ISCHIUM,** AND **PUBIS.** SAURISCHIAN DINOSAURS HAD THEIR **PUBIS BONE** POINTING **DOWN** AND **FORWARD.**

Velociraptor was a Saurischian dinosaur. It was a fierce and agile carnivore of the Late Cretaceous Period.

SAURISCHIAN DINOSAURS INCLUDE ALL THE **CARNIVORES** AND THE **SAUROPODS.** THE SAUROPODS WERE **HERBIVOROUS** DINOSAURS WITH VERY **LONG NECKS** AND **MASSIVE BODIES.** NO MATTER WHAT THEY **LOOKED LIKE** ON THE OUTSIDE AND WHAT THEIR **HABITS** WERE, **SAURISCHIANS** HAD THEIR HIP BONES **SHAPED** AND **POSITIONED** THE **SAME WAY.**

Diplodocus was a Sauropod living during the Late Jurassic Period. Unlike Velociraptor, Diplodocus was a herbivore.

ORNITHISCHIAN DINOSAURS

IN **ORNITHISCHIAN DINOSAURS** THE **PUBIS BONE** IS POINTING **DOWN** AND **BACKWARD**. THIS **HIP BONE ARRANGEMENT** IS VERY **SIMILAR** TO THE ONE OF **MODERN BIRDS**.

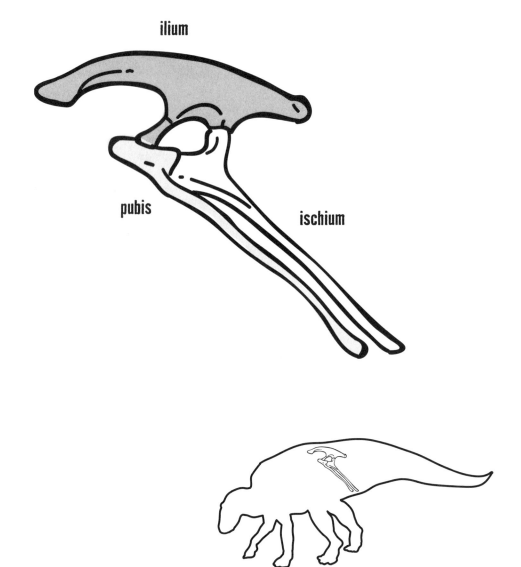

ilium

pubis

ischium

INTERESTINGLY, **ORNITHISCHIAN DINOSAURS** ARE NOT THE **ANCESTORS** OF **BIRDS**. **BIRDS** DESCEND FROM **SAURISCHIAN DINOSAURS**.

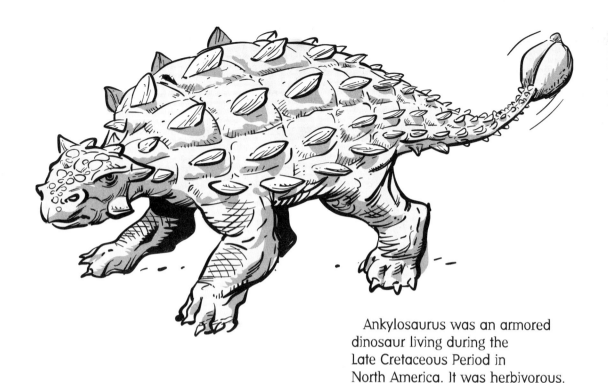

Ankylosaurus was an armored
dinosaur living during the
Late Cretaceous Period in
North America. It was herbivorous.

DESPITE THEIR **GREAT PHYSICAL DIFFERENCES**, ALL **ORNITHISCHIAN DINOSAURS** WERE **HERBIVOROUS.**

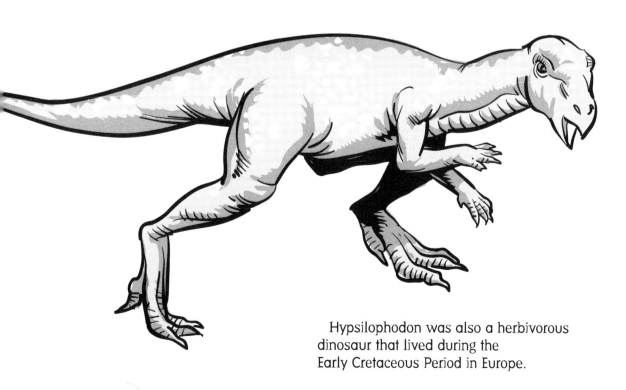

Hypsilophodon was also a herbivorous
dinosaur that lived during the
Early Cretaceous Period in Europe.

WHEN DINOSAURS LIVED

MYA MEANS MILLION YEARS AGO

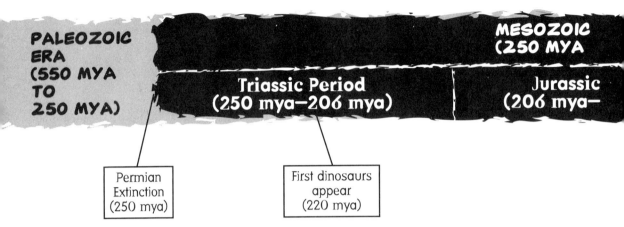

PALEOZOIC ERA (550 MYA TO 250 MYA)		MESOZOIC (250 MYA
	Triassic Period (250 mya–206 mya)	Jurassic (206 mya–

Permian Extinction (250 mya)

First dinosaurs appear (220 mya)

THE **SPAN** OF **LIFE** ON OUR PLANET IS DIVIDED INTO THREE **ERAS:** **PALEOZOIC, MESOZOIC,** AND **CENOZOIC.**

PALEOZOIC MEANS "**ANCIENT LIFE.**" DURING THIS ERA, **LIFE** FIRST **APPEARED** ON **EARTH.** IT EVOLVED AND DIVERSIFIED INTO MANY **SPECIES** LIKE **FISH** AND **REPTILES.** THE **PERMIAN EXTINCTION,** DURING WHICH **90%** OF **ANIMALS** AND **PLANTS** DIED, **MARKED** THE **END** OF THE **PALEOZOIC ERA.**

ERA TO 65 MYA)		CENOZOIC ERA (65 MYA TO TODAY)
Period 144 mya)	Cretaceous Period (144 mya65 mya)	

K/T Event (65 mya)

You are here (today)

MESOZOIC MEANS **"MIDDLE LIFE."** THIS ERA IS ALSO CALLED THE **"AGE OF DINOSAURS."** IT'S DIVIDED INTO **THREE PERIODS** CALLED **TRIASSIC, JURASSIC,** AND **CRETACEOUS.**

DINOSAURS EVOLVED DURING THE **TRIASSIC PERIOD.**

AT THE **END** OF THE **MESOZOIC ERA** A MASS EXTINCTION OCCURRED. IT KILLED **80%** OF **LIFE,** INCLUDING ALL **MARINE REPTILES, FLYING REPTILES** AND **DINOSAURS.** THIS MASS EXTINCTION IS CALLED THE **K/T EVENT.**

CENOZOIC MEANS **"RECENT LIFE."** DURING THIS ERA, **MAMMALS,** WHICH HAD EVOLVED DURING THE **MESOZOIC,** TOOK OVER THE PLANET. **TWO MILLION YEARS AGO,** THE **FIRST HUMANOIDS** APPEARED. HUMANOIDS WERE THE **PREDECESSORS** OF **HUMANS.**

COELOPHYSIS

see-lo-fise-is   *"Hollow Form"*

SCALE

IN 1947, PALEONTOLOGISTS FOUND A **CEMETERY** OF **FOSSILIZED COELOPHYSIS** IN **GHOST RANCH,** NEW MEXICO. THE FOSSILS SHOWED THESE DINOAURS WERE **CANNIBALS**— IN FACT, THEY **ATE** THEIR OWN **BABIES** WHEN FOOD WAS **SCARCE!**

TRIASSIC ● **JURASSIC** ● **CRETACEOUS**

WHEN PALEONTOLOGISTS FOUND **COELOPHYSIS,** THEY NAMED IT **RIOARRIBASAURUS.** IT TURNED OUT THAT 40 YEARS EARLIER, IN 1889, **EDWARD DRINKER COPE** HAD ALREADY NAMED IT **COELOPHYSIS.** THE **INTERNATIONAL COMMISSION ON ZOOLOGICAL NOMENCLATURE** DECIDED TO DROP RIOARRIBASAURUS, THE **NEWER NAME,** AND USE **COELOPHYSIS** INSTEAD.

LENGTH: 9 FEET
WEIGHT: 50 LBS

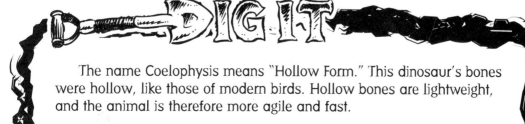

DIG IT

The name Coelophysis means "Hollow Form." This dinosaur's bones were hollow, like those of modern birds. Hollow bones are lightweight, and the animal is therefore more agile and fast.

DISCOVER

It's not always the person who discovers a dinosaur that gets to name it. This is generally up to the paleontologist who studies and "describes" the discovery.

The Flagstones are about to make a great discovery...

They find an intriguing rock, and they decide to contact the local museum of natural history.

A paleontologist organizes an expedition to the location of the Flagstones' discovery. A big fossilized skeleton is retreived and brought back to the museum lab.

After studying the fossils, the paleontologist announces what she has learned about the discovery. She describes the bones in detail. She explains what she has noticed by comparing these fossils with the ones of similar and well-known animals. If she concludes that the bones belong to an unknown dinosaur, she gets to name it.

Watch the "Dig It!" sections. Sometimes they mention the dinosaur discoverers, other times they mention the paleontologist who described them.

PLATEOSAURUS

plat-ee-oh-sawr-us "*Broad Lizard*"

THE NAME **PLATEOSAURUS,** WHICH IS GREEK FOR **"BROAD LIZARD,"** WAS GIVEN TO THIS DINOSAUR BECAUSE OF ITS **LARGE SIZE.**

PLATEOSAURUS HAD **FIVE CLAWS** ON EACH OF ITS HANDS.

TRIASSIC • **JURASSIC** • **CRETACEOUS**

LENGTH: 30 FEET
WEIGHT: 4 TONS

SCALE

PLATEOSAURUS WAS **QUADRUPEDAL,** BUT IF **ATTACKED,** IT RAN AWAY ON ITS **TWO BACK LEGS.**

ITS **TAIL** WAS AS **LONG** AS ITS **BODY.**

Plateosaurus lived in HERDS. Many fossils of this dinosaur have been found buried together.

DIG IT

Plateosaurus was first described by German paleontologist Hermann Von Meyer in 1837. Fossils have been found in Germany, France, and Switzerland.

MUSSAURUS

mus-oh-rus   *"Mouse Lizard"*

WHEN **MUSSAURUS** WAS FIRST FOUND IN 1979 IN **ARGENTINA**, IT WAS THE **SMALLEST DINOSAUR** EVER—ONLY **EIGHT INCHES LONG!** SO IT WAS NAMED **"MOUSE LIZARD."** BUT, A CLOSER LOOK REVEALED THE FINDINGS WERE **BABY DINOSAURS,** AND THE **ADULTS** MIGHT HAVE BEEN **BIGGER.** BUT NO FOSSILS OF **ADULT MUSSAURUS** HAVE BEEN FOUND SO FAR!

LENGTH: 10 FEET
WEIGHT: 260 LBS

Mussaurus was first described by Argentinian paleontologists Jose Bonaparte and Martin Vince in 1979.

Mussaurus was a herbivore and fed on FERNS and CYCADS (trees similar to palms).

MUSSAURUS RETAINS A **RECORD:** THE FOSSILS FOUND IN 1979 WERE THE **SMALLEST** EVER FOUND OF A **BABY DINOSAUR!** THE **DIMENSIONS** AND SCALE OF AN **ADULT MUSSAURUS** ARE **APPROXIMATE.**

SCALE

TRIASSIC • JURASSIC • CRETACEOUS

PREHISTORIC
F.A.Q.S

FREQUENTLY ASKED QUESTIONS

DID DINOSAURS SWIM OR FLY?

Neither. Only certain reptiles could swim, like Ichthyosaurus. And only certain reptiles could fly, like Pterodactylus. Some dinosaurs, though, had feathers and eventually evolved into birds.

DID DINOSAURS ALL LIVE AT THE SAME TIME?

Some dinosaurs were extinct by the time others appeared. For example, by the time T. Rex was ruling the Late Cretaceous Period, Apatosaurus had already been extinct for 80 million years!

DID PEOPLE AND DINOSAURS LIVE TOGETHER?

No, they didn't. Some mammals coexisted with dinosaurs, but they were mostly small rodents. About 60 million years separates the extinction of dinosaurs and the appearance of the first hominids (ancestors of humans).

WERE ALL HUGE PREHISTORIC ANIMALS DINOSAURS?

Some dinosaurs were huge, but some reptiles were pretty big, too. For example, Shonisaurus was a 49-foot-long marine reptile that lived during the Late Triassic Period. Even mammals could be massive, like Basilosaurus, an extinct whale that measured 82 feet long! That's as long as 20 kids!

TYRANNOSAURUS YUKs!

1. WHAT DO YOU CALL A REALLY **UNEXCITING DINOSAUR?**

—A DINO-**BORE!**

2. WHAT DO YOU SAY WHEN YOU AND YOUR FRIEND **TIP-TOE PAST** A **T. REX?**

—"DOYOUTHINKHE-**SAURUS?"**

Z-Z-Z

3. WHAT **DINOSAUR** WOULD MAKE A GOOD **POLICE OFFICER?**

—TRICERA-**COPS!**

4. WHERE DOES **HETERODONTOSAURUS** GO ON **VACATION?**

—TO THE DINO-**SHORE!**

5. WHAT DO YOU GET WHEN YOU **CROSS** A **DINOSAUR** WITH A **CAR ACCIDENT?**

—TYRANNOSAURUS **WRECKS!**

6. WHAT DO YOU CALL A **DINOSAUR** THAT WEARS **ALL PLAID?**

—TYRANNOSAURUS **CHECKS!**

ALLOSAURUS

al-uh-sawr-us **"Different Lizard"**

When Othniel Marsh first described Allosaurus' fossils, he observed that the vertebrae were different from similar dinosaurs. They had indentations. He named it Allosaurus, which means "Different Lizard."

Marsh thought these indentations would make Allosaurus lighter and more agile, but also weaker, so he named the species "fragile."

When more Allosaurus bones were found, it was clear that Marsh had been looking at damaged fossils, but the name stuck.

ALLOSAURUS' WEAPONS INCLUDED A **THREE-FOOT-LONG HEAD** ARMED WITH **FOUR-INCH-LONG FANGS,** AND **SIX-INCH-LONG CLAWS** ON ITS **HANDS!**

SOME BELIEVE **ALLOSAURUS** HUNTED IN **PACKS. A PACK** WOULD HAVE BEEN ABLE TO **KILL** DINOSAURS MUCH **BIGGER** THAN ALLOSAURUS, LIKE **DIPLODOCUS** AND **APATOSAURUS.** AFTER KILLING THE PREY, THE **PACK** WOULD HAVE **SHARED** THE **FOOD.**

ALLOSAURUS

ALLOSAURUS' TAIL WAS STRAIGHT AND PARALLEL TO THE GROUND, BALANCING ITS HEAVY HEAD.

SCALE

HEIGHT: 17 FEET

WEIGHT: 5 TONS

LENGTH: 37 FEET

Footnote: Allosaurus had "gastralia," belly ribs that supported its guts. They were not attached to its spine, but were embedded in its skin.

OME SCIENTISTS BELIEVE **ALLOSAURUS** WAS A **SCAVENGER.** OTHERS BELIEVE IT WAS A **HUNTER.** BUT WHAT'S THE **DIFFERENCE** BETWEEN A **HUNTER** AND A **SCAVENGER?**

A **HUNTER** PURSUES **LIVE ANIMALS,** AND NEEDS TO **RUN** AFTER **ITS PREY.** A **SCAVENGER** FEEDS ON **ANIMALS** THAT ARE ALREADY **DEAD,** AND DOES NOT NEED TO GIVE **CHASE.**

THE MAJORITY OF **SCIENTISTS** BELIEVE **ALLOSAURUS** WAS A **SCAVENGER** RATHER THAN A **HUNTER.** IT AVOIDED **RUNNING** BECAUSE ITS **TINY HANDS** AND **ARMS** WOULD MAKE IT **DIFFICULT** TO **GET UP** IF IT **FELL.**

MANY **ALLOSAURUS BONES** WITH **HEALED CRACKS** IN THEM HAVE BEEN FOUND. THIS LEADS SOME OTHER **PALEONTOLOGISTS** TO BELIEVE THAT **ALLOSAURUS** WAS A **HUNTER** ABLE TO WITHSTAND A **TUMBLE** OR **TWO.**

Footnote: Allosaurus fossils have been found in North America and Australia, indicating, that at one time, these two continents were joined.

BRACHIOSAURUS

brak-ee-o-sawr-us   *"Arm Lizard"*

PALEONTOLOGISTS USED TO THINK **BRACHIOSAURUS** LIVED IN THE **SEA**, GRAZING ON **SEAWEED** ON THE **OCEAN FLOOR**. WHEN **BRACHIOSAURUS** NEEDED TO **BREATHE**, ITS **NOSTRILS** WERE CONVENIENTLY POSITIONED ON **TOP** OF ITS **HEAD**. **BRACHIOSAURUS** COULD RAISE ITS HEAD ABOVE **WATER**, LIKE A **SUBMARINE PERISCOPE**.

BUT THIS **THEORY** WAS LATER **ABANDONED**. **PALEONTOLOGISTS** REALIZED THAT THE **PRESSURE** OF THE **WATER** WOULD HAVE MADE IT **EXTREMELY HARD** FOR **BRACHIOSAURUS** TO **MOVE**. IN FACT, IT WOULD HAVE **CONSTRAINED** ITS **LUNGS**, MAKING BREATHING **IMPOSSIBLE**.

SCALE

TRIASSIC ● **JURASSIC** ● **CRETACEOUS**

LENGTH: 80 FEET
WEIGHT: 70 TONS

THE NAME "ARM LIZARD" WAS GIVEN TO BRACHIOSAURUS BY PALEONTOLOGIST ELMER SAMUEL RIGGS IN 1903. HE CHOSE THIS NAME BECAUSE BRACHIOSAURUS' FRONT LEGS WERE SO MUCH LONGER THAN ITS BACK ONES.

Footnote: Brachiosaurus' fossils have been found in the United States in Colorado; and in Africa in Tanzania and Algeria.

DIG IT

Between 1907 and 1911, Dr. Werner Janensch, a curator for the Berlin Museum, led an expedition to Tendaguru, Tanzania (Africa). This place was known for being rich in fossils.

The huge and expensive expedition unearthed the largest and most complete Brachiosaurus skeleton in the world. It's still exhibited in the Humboldt Museum in Berlin!

UNSOLVED MYSTERIES

"NESSIE"

Although extinct for millions of years, prehistoric animals
seem to reappear in the most unlikely places!

THE **LOCH NESS MONSTER**, BETTER KNOWN AS **NESSIE**, IS A **MARINE REPTILE** RUMORED TO BE LIVING IN THE WATERS OF **LOCH NESS**, A **LAKE** IN **SCOTLAND**. PEOPLE WHO CLAIM TO HAVE SEEN **NESSIE** SAY SHE LOOKS LIKE A BIG **PLESIOSAURUS**, WITH A **LONG NECK** AND **FINS**...BUT THESE ANIMALS LIVED MORE THAT **200 MILLION YEARS AGO** AND SUPPOSEDLY HAVE BEEN **EXTINCT** FOR OVER **65 MILLION YEARS!**

THE **LEGEND,** STARTED IN THE **MIDDLE AGES**, BECAME KNOWN **WORLDWIDE** ON APRIL 14, 1933. THE OWNERS OF A NEARBY PUB DECLARED TO HAVE SEEN A **VERY BIG, PLESIOSAURUS-LIKE ANIMAL** PLUNGING INTO THE **LAKE!**

ON APRIL 19, 1934, **COLONEL ROBERT WILSON** TOOK A **PICTURE** THAT BECAME **NESSIE'S** MOST FAMOUS IMAGE. HOWEVER, IN 1993, **CHRISTIAN SPURLING** CONFESSED ON HIS DEATHBED THAT HE HAD BEEN HIRED, ALONG WITH **WILSON**, BY A **NEWSPAPER**. THEY NEEDED TO FIND **EVIDENCE** OF THE **MONSTER**.

IN ORDER TO POCKET THE NEWSPAPER **REWARD**, THEY CREATED **NESSIE** OUT OF A **TOY SUBMARINE**, AND TOOK A **PHOTO** OF IT.

DESPITE THE MANY **SCIENTIFIC SEARCHES** CONDUCTED, NO DEFINITE PROOF, LIKE A **PHOTOGRAPH** OR A **VIDEO**, WAS EVER COLLECTED. SO THE **MYSTERY** REMAINS: IS THERE A **PLESIOSAUR** CALLED **NESSIE** LIVING AT THE BOTTOM OF **LOCH NESS?**

STEGOSAURUS

steg-oh-sawr-us   *"Covered Lizard"*

STEGOSAURUS WEIGHED **3.5 TONS**, BUT ITS **BRAIN** WAS ONLY AS **BIG** AS A **WALNUT!** THIS **DISPROPORTION** PROBABLY MADE STEGOSAURUS THE **DUMBEST DINOSAUR** THAT EVER LIVED!
    DESPITE THIS, STEGOSAURUS SURVIVED FOR MORE THAN **50 MILLION YEARS,** WHICH IS **A LOT LONGER** THAN THE **HUMAN SPECIES** HAS LIVED UP TO TODAY!

SCALE

TRIASSIC   JURASSIC   CRETACEOUS

STEGOSAURUS HAD **ROWS** OF **PLATES** ON ITS **BACK**. PALEONTOLOGISTS THINK STEGOSAURUS' PLATES REGULATED ITS **TEMPERATURE**. FOSSILS SHOW THE PLATES WERE FILLED WITH **BLOOD VESSELS**. WHEN IT WAS **HOT**, STEGOSAURUS TURNED ITS PLATES AWAY FROM THE **SUN**. THE BLOOD COOLED DOWN BY **RUNNING THROUGH** THE PLATES. THEN, THE **COOL BLOOD**, RUNNING THROUGH STEGOSAURUS' **BODY**, LOWERED ITS **TEMPERATURE**. WHEN IT WAS **COLD**, STEGOSAURUS TURNED ITS PLATES TOWARD THE **SUN**. THE BLOOD **WARMED UP**, AND WARMED ITS **BODY**, TOO.

THE **PLATES** WERE PROBABLY USED IN OTHER WAYS, TOO. THEY KEPT AWAY **PREDATORS**, ATTRACTED MATES, AND SHOWED OFF **STEGOSAURUS' RANK** WITHIN ITS **HERD**.

DIG IT

In 1992, an almost complete skeleton of Stegosaurus was found in Colorado. For the first time since 1877 (when the first Stegosaurus was found) paleontologists learned how Stegosaurus' plates were attached to its back.

STEGOSAURUS

STEGOSAURUS' TAIL BORE **FOUR SPIKES,** WHICH WERE **TWO FEET LONG** EACH. THEY WERE VERY LIKELY USED TO FIGHT OFF **ENEMIES.** STEGOSAURUS COULD **SWING** ITS **TAIL** AND **WHACK** A **PREDATOR** WITH ITS **DANGEROUS SPINES!**

IT WAS POSSIBLE FOR **STEGOSAURUS** TO STAND ON ITS **TAIL** AND **BACK LEGS** TO REACH **HIGHER PLANTS.**

LENGTH: 30 FEET
HEIGHT: 9 FEET
WEIGHT: 3.5 TONS

STEGOSAURUS' BACK LEGS WERE LONGER AND STRAIGHTER THAN THE FRONT ONES. IN THIS TILTED POSITION, ITS HEAD WAS CLOSER TO THE GROUND AND TO STEGOSAURUS' FOOD.

STEGOSAURUS' PUNY HEAD WAS ONLY ONE FOOT LONG AND STOOD THREE FEET FROM THE GROUND! IT HAD A BEAK AND SMALL CHEEK TEETH TO CHEW PLANTS.

STEGOSAURUS' BACK FEET HAD ONLY THREE TOES, WHILE ITS FRONT ONES HAD FIVE TOES.

BECAUSE STEGOSAURUS' BRAIN WAS TOO SMALL, IT WASN'T ABLE TO ACHIEVE FULL BODY MOBILITY OF THE BACK LEGS AND TAIL.

STEGOSAURUS HAD A GANGLION, A NERVE CENTER, LOCATED IN ITS BACK, NEAR ITS REAR. THE GANGLION COORDINATED STEGOSAURUS' BACK LEGS AND TAIL MOVEMENTS.

THE GANGLION WAS BIGGER THAN THE BRAIN. AT FIRST, PALEONTOLOGISTS ACTUALLY THOUGHT THAT STEGOSAURUS HAD TWO BRAINS!

Footnote: The biggest plates on Stegosaurus' back were 2.5 feet long. They were made of bone and covered with skin.

MAMENCHISAURUS

mah-men-chee-sawr-us **"Lizard from Mamenchi"**

MAMENCHISAURUS OWES ITS NAME TO **MAMENCHI**, A PLACE IN **CHINA** WERE IT WAS FIRST UNEARTHED. THE **DISCOVERY** WAS MADE IN **1957** BY THE GREAT CHINESE PALEONTOLOGIST **YANG ZHONG JIAN** (CHUNG-CHIEN YOUNG).

SCALE

LENGTH:
80 FEET
WEIGHT:
12 TONS

TRIASSIC • JURASSIC • CRETACEOUS

MAMENCHISAURUS HAD THE **LONGEST NECK** OF ALL DINOSAURS: IT MEASURED **46 FEET,** HALF THE **LENGTH** OF THE WHOLE **DINOSAUR!**

THE **NECK** WAS SUPPORTED BY **19 VERTEBRAE,** THE **MOST** EVER IN ANY DINOSAUR'S **NECK!**

STRUTS MADE THE VERTEBRAE **STRONG,** BUT NOT VERY **FLEXIBLE.** MAMENCHISAURUS COULDN'T **BEND** ITS **NECK** VERY MUCH, AND PROBABLY KEPT IT ALMOST **STRAIGHT,** WITH ITS **HEAD** LOW AND NEAR THE **GROUND.**

DIG IT

Mamenchisaurus' head needed to be small and light, otherwise its long neck would not have been able to support the weight.

COMPSOGNATHUS

komp-sog-nay-us   *"Delicate Jaw"*

COMPSOGNATHUS AND ARCHAEOPTERYX, A BIRD ANCESTOR, LIVED IN EUROPE DURING THE LATE JURASSIC PERIOD. THEY WERE RELATED BECAUSE THEIR BONES WERE VERY SIMILAR AND THEY WERE BOTH APPROXIMATELY THE SAME SIZE. SOMETIMES RESEARCHERS MISTAKE ONE FOR THE OTHER.

DIG IT

Compsognathus was one of the smallest dinosaurs ever. In fact, it wasn't much bigger than a chicken!

A COMPSOGNATHUS WAS ONCE FOUND WITH AN **ANIMAL** IN ITS **BELLY**. PALEONTOLOGISTS THOUGHT **COMPSOGNATHUS** GAVE BIRTH TO **LIVE YOUNG**, AS OPPOSED TO **LAYING EGGS** LIKE OTHER DINOSAURS.

IT TURNED OUT THE LITTLE **ANIMAL** WAS A **BAVARISAURUS**, A PREHISTORIC **LIZARD**, THAT **COMPSOGNATHUS** HAD **EATEN** JUST **BEFORE DYING!**

COMPSOGNATHUS HAD ONLY **TWO FINGERS** ON ITS HANDS, BUT IT HAD **THREE TOES** WITH **CLAWS** AND A **FOURTH TOE** POINTING **BACKWARDS.**

COMPSOGNATHUS LIVED ON **DESERT ISLANDS** THAT USED TO BE WHERE **GERMANY** IS TODAY.

SCALE

LENGTH: 4 - 5 FEET
WEIGHT: 6 LBS

TRIASSIC   JURASSIC   CRETACEOUS

Many animals that are now extinct lived at the same time as dinosaurs. Here are some of the weirder-looking ones!

ARCHAEOPTERYX

ar-kee-op-ter-iks   "Ancient Wing"

ARCHAEOPTERYX WAS A **BIRD ANCESTOR** THAT LIVED DURING THE **LATE JURASSIC PERIOD**, AT THE SAME TIME AS **COMPSOGNATHUS** AND **MEGALOSAURUS**. THE FIRST **ARCHAEOPTERYX FOSSILS** WERE FOUND IN A **LIMESTONE QUARRY** IN 1891 IN **SONHOFEN, GERMANY**.

ARCHAEOPTERYX HAD A **MIX** OF **DINOSAUR** AND **BIRD FEATURES**. IT WAS AS **BIG** AS A **PIGEON** AND **FED** ON **INSECTS**.

ONE OF ITS **BIRD CHARACTERISTICS** WAS THE ABILITY TO **LEAP, FLAP,** AND **GLIDE,** ALTHOUGH IT COULD **NOT FLY**.

ARCHAEOPTERYX HAD A **WISHBONE** AND **HOLLOW BONES**, JUST LIKE **MODERN BIRDS**. IT ALSO HAD **FEATHERS**. SOMETIMES, WHEN AN ARCHAEOPTERYX **DIED** AND **FOSSILIZED,** ITS **FEATHERS** LEFT AN **IMPRESSION** ON THE SURROUNDING **ROCKS**.

ARCHAEOPTERYX HAD **CLAWS** ON ITS HANDS THAT WERE USEFUL FOR **CLIMBING** ON **TREES**.

JUST LIKE SOME **DINOSAURS,** ARCHAEOPTERYX HAD **LONG LEGS** AND WAS PROBABLY A **GOOD RUNNER**.

CERATOSAURUS

keh-rat-oh-sawr-us "Horned Lizard"

ERATOSAURUS WAS NAMED BY AMERICAN PALEONTOLOGIST OTHNIEL MARSH IN 1844.
CERATOSAURUS OWES ITS NAME TO THE HORN ON TOP OF ITS **NOSE**. IN FACT, **"KERAS"** MEANS **"HORN"** IN **GREEK**.

SCALE

TRIASSIC   JURASSIC   CRETACEOUS

CERATOSAURUS WAS A VERY **INTELLIGENT** AND **FIERCE PREDATOR.** SOME PALEONTOLOGISTS BELIEVE **CERATOSAURUS** HUNTED IN **PACKS** LIKE MODERN **WOLVES.**

THE **HORN** ON **CERATOSAURUS' NOSE** DOESN'T SEEM TO HAVE HAD A **PURPOSE.** IT WAS TOO **SMALL** FOR **KILLING PREY,** AND **CERATOSAURUS' CLAWS** AND **TEETH** WERE MUCH MORE EFFICIENT **WEAPONS.** PALEONTOLOGISTS THINK CERATOSAURUS USED ITS **HORN** FOR **SELF-DEFENSE** WITHIN ITS OWN **PACK.**

Fossils of Ceratosaurus have been found in Tanzania and the United States.

Sir Richard Owen

Sir Richard Owen (1804-1892) was the inventor of the word "dinosaur." He was a British professor at the Royal College of Surgeons, founder of the division of Natural History for the British Museum, and the tutor of Queen Victoria's children.

Owen studied dinosaur fossils, many submitted to him by the British physician Gideon Mantell (see following page). Owen discovered that the fossils didn't belong to any known animal of the time. He decided he had discovered a new group. He named it "terrible lizards," or "dinosaurs."

Despite his success as a scientists, Owen often tried to take credit for Mantell's work. He even attempted to prevent Mantell from being recognized by the Royal Society for his work and dedication to paleontology.

Owen was a very eccentric man. In 1853, he commissioned sculptor Benjamin Waterhouse Hawkins to build a life-size model of Iguanodon. Then he invited fellow members of the British Association for the Advancement of Science to have dinner with him inside it.

Gideon Mantell

Gideon Mantell (1790-1852) was a British physician. In 1820, his wife Maryann found some fossilized teeth while riding her horse in the countryside. Mantell noticed they resembled the teeth of an iguana, a tropical lizard, but were much bigger.

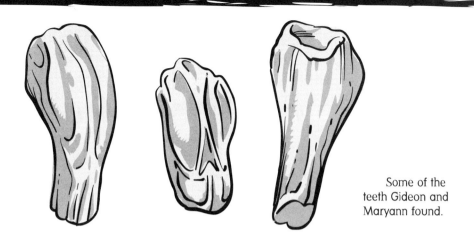

Some of the teeth Gideon and Maryann found.

Mantell decided the teeth belonged to an unknown animal. He named it "Iguanodon," or "Iguana Tooth." The scientific community scorned his discovery. Sir Richard Owen (see previous page) declared that Mantell, a mere country doctor, had just discovered some very common rhinoceros teeth.

Later, after studying more fossils provided to him by Mantell, Owen changed his mind. He agreed that at one point in time, some very strange-looking animals, the dinosaurs, roamed the earth.

Mantell's passion for fossils bordered on obsession. By the time he had finally proved to the scientific community that the teeth he had found weren't those of a rhino, his wife and children had moved out of his house and he was broke.

Mantell died in 1852, after 10 years of persistent back pains due to a carriage accident. Despite being physically crippled, Mantell never stopped his scientific research.

CAMARASAURUS

kam-ar-ah-sawr-us   *"Lizard with Chambers"*

CAMARASAURUS OWES ITS NAME TO ITS **VERTEBRAE** (THE **BONES** OF ITS **SPINE**). THEY HAD **"CHAMBERS"** (MEANING THEY WERE **HOLLOW**), IN FACT, **"KAMARA"** MEANS **"CHAMBER"** IN **GREEK.**

THE **VERTEBRAE** WERE LIGHTER BUT **STURDY** ENOUGH TO **SUPPORT** THIS DINOSAUR'S **IMMENSE WEIGHT.**

SCALE

LENGTH: 60 FEET
WEIGHT: 20 TONS

TRIASSIC   JURASSIC   CRETACEOUS

DESPITE ITS **IMPRESSIVE SIZE,** CAMARASAURUS WAS ONE OF THE **SMALLER** MEMBERS OF THE **SAUROPODS,** WHICH INCLUDED THE MASSIVE **BRACHIOSAURUS** AND HUGE **APATOSAURUS.**

CAMARASAURUS' SKULL HAD BIG **OPENINGS** FOR ITS **NOSTRILS.** THIS LED SOME SCIENTISTS TO THINK **CAMARASAURUS** HAD A **TRUNK** LIKE AN **ELEPHANT!**

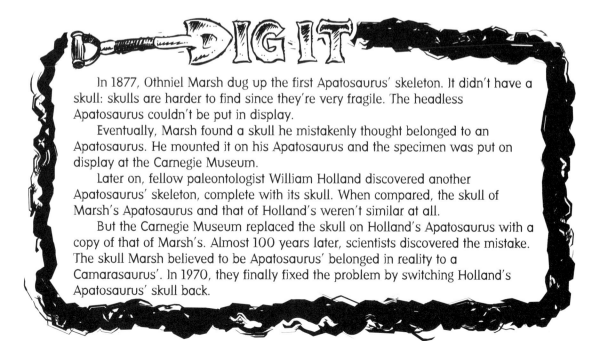

DIG IT

In 1877, Othniel Marsh dug up the first Apatosaurus' skeleton. It didn't have a skull: skulls are harder to find since they're very fragile. The headless Apatosaurus couldn't be put in display.

Eventually, Marsh found a skull he mistakenly thought belonged to an Apatosaurus. He mounted it on his Apatosaurus and the specimen was put on display at the Carnegie Museum.

Later on, fellow paleontologist William Holland discovered another Apatosaurus' skeleton, complete with its skull. When compared, the skull of Marsh's Apatosaurus and that of Holland's weren't similar at all.

But the Carnegie Museum replaced the skull on Holland's Apatosaurus with a copy of that of Marsh's. Almost 100 years later, scientists discovered the mistake. The skull Marsh believed to be Apatosaurus' belonged in reality to a Camarasaurus'. In 1970, they finally fixed the problem by switching Holland's Apatosaurus' skull back.

HETERODONTOSAURUS

het-er-oh-dont-oh-sawr-us "Different Teeth Lizard"

HETERODONTOSAURUS HAD **THREE** DIFFERENT KINDS OF **TEETH**. ALL THE OTHER **DINOSAURS** HAD **ONLY ONE** KIND. THIS PECULIARITY IS REFLECTED IN ITS **NAME**.

HETERODONTOSAURUS WAS ONLY AS **BIG** AS A **CAT!**

SCALE

LENGTH: 3 FEET
WEIGHT: 6 LBS

TRIASSIC ● JURASSIC ● CRETACEOUS

ETERODONTOSAURUS' UPPER FRONT TEETH WERE VERY **SMALL** AND **POINTY**, AND WERE USED TO **SHRED FOLIAGE**. THEY HAD **FOUR BIG FANGS**, WHICH ARE USUALLY FOUND IN **CARNIVORES**. SINCE THE **HETERODONTOSAURUS** WAS **HERBIVOROUS**, SCIENTISTS ARE NOT SURE WHAT THESE **TEETH** WERE USED FOR. MAYBE HETERODONTOSAURUS' **"DRACULA LOOK"** SCARED AWAY **PREDATORS**. FINALLY, **HETERODONTOSAURUS** HAD **CHEEK TEETH**, USED TO **CHEW** ITS **FOOD**.

Footnote: Heterodontosaurus' legs were more than a third longer than its arms.

SCELIDOSAURUS

skel-ide-oh-sawr-us   *"Hind-Leg Lizard"*

SCELIDOSAURUS' NAME REFERS TO THIS DINOSAUR'S VERY **LONG** AND **STRONG BACK LEGS.** ITS **HIPS** WERE VERY **HIGH** AND **MASSIVE,** WHILE ITS **HEAD** WAS VERY SMALL.

DIG IT

Scelidosaurus was described for the first time by Sir Richard Owen in 1859. Owen was also the inventor of the word "dinosaur."

JUST LIKE ALL THE OTHER **ARMORED** DINOSAURS, **SCELIDOSAURUS** HAD A VERY SMALL **HEAD** AND A **TINY BRAIN.** THIS DINOSAUR ATE **VEGETATION** AND **ROOTS** IT TORE OFF WITH ITS **BEAK.**

SCELIDOSAURUS' BACK WAS COVERED WITH A **BONY SKIN** AND **STUDS.** THIS **ARMOR** SPANNED FROM ITS **HEAD** TO THE TIP OF ITS **TAIL,** AND PROTECTED **SCELIDOSAURUS** AGAINST ITS **ENEMIES.**

← SCALE →

LENGTH:
15 FEET
HEIGHT:
5 FEET
WEIGHT:
500 LBS

TRIASSIC ● JURASSIC ● CRETACEOUS

BAROSAURUS

bahr-oh-sawr-us   *"Heavy Lizard"*

BAROSAURUS WAS A **HUGE** ANIMAL WITH A **30-FOOT-LONG NECK** AND A **43-FOOT-LONG TAIL** THAT WAS ALMOST AS **WIDE** AS A **BASKETBALL COURT!**

LENGTH: 90 FEET
WEIGHT: 10 TONS

TRIASSIC ● **JURASSIC** ● **CRETACEOUS**

JUST LIKE **DIPLODOCUS**, BAROSAURUS' VERTEBRAE (NECK BONES) WERE **HOLLOW, LIGHT,** AND **STRONG**. THESE TWO **DINOSAURS** WERE SO **SIMILAR** THAT IT'S VERY **DIFFICULT** TO TELL THEIR FOSSILS **APART**.

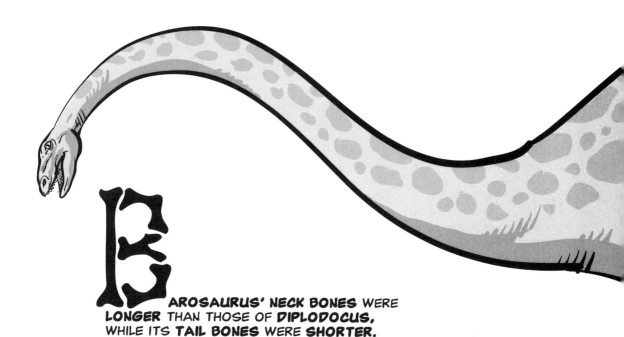

BAROSAURUS' NECK BONES WERE **LONGER** THAN THOSE OF **DIPLODOCUS**, WHILE ITS **TAIL BONES** WERE **SHORTER**.

BAROSAURUS' NECK BONES COULD BE AS LONG AS **THREE FEET!** ONE OF ITS **VERTEBRAE** COULD BE AS **LONG** AS YOU ARE **TALL!**

← SCALE →

DIG IT

Barosaurus' fossils have been found in places like Tanzania, Africa, and South Dakota.

CHASMOSAURUS

kaz-mo-sawr-us   *"Lizard with Skull Openings"*

CHASMOSAURUS HAD A **FRILL** MADE OF **BONE** AND COVERED WITH **SKIN.** THE FRILL PROTECTED CHASMOSAURUS' DELICATE **NECK** FROM ITS **ENEMIES' BITE.**

CHASMOSAURUS HAD **THREE FACIAL HORNS** TO DEFEND **ITSELF** WITH WHEN **ASSAILED.** CHASMOSAURUS WOULD **CHARGE** ITS ATTACKER **HEAD DOWN,** LIKE A BULL OR A RHINO.

CHASMOSAURUS ALSO USED ITS **FRILL** AND **HORNS** TO FIGHT THE **OTHER MALES** OF THE **HERD** DURING MATING SEASON.

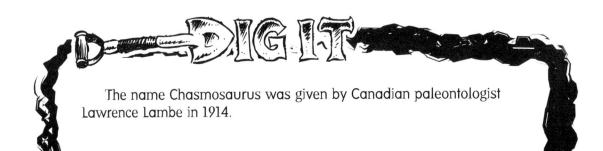

DIG IT

The name Chasmosaurus was given by Canadian paleontologist Lawrence Lambe in 1914.

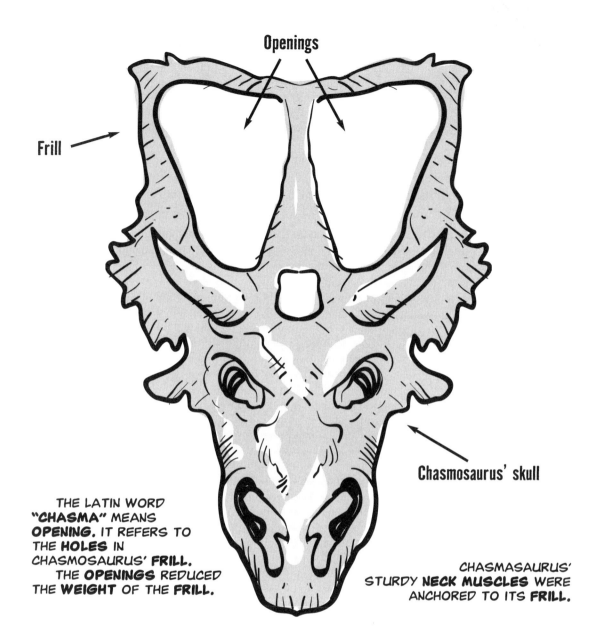

Openings

Frill

Chasmosaurus' skull

THE LATIN WORD "CHASMA" MEANS OPENING. IT REFERS TO THE HOLES IN CHASMOSAURUS' FRILL.
THE OPENINGS REDUCED THE WEIGHT OF THE FRILL.

CHASMASAURUS' STURDY NECK MUSCLES WERE ANCHORED TO ITS FRILL.

SCALE

LENGTH:
16 FEET
WEIGHT:
3 TONS

TRIASSIC ● JURASSIC ● CRETACEOUS

EARTH BOUND

The earth's crust is made of continents and oceans that lay on top of the mantle. The mantle is made of hot and fluid magma. The continents slowly slide on the mantle, changing the look of our planet. The Earth today appears very different from the way it was at the Age of Dinosaurs!

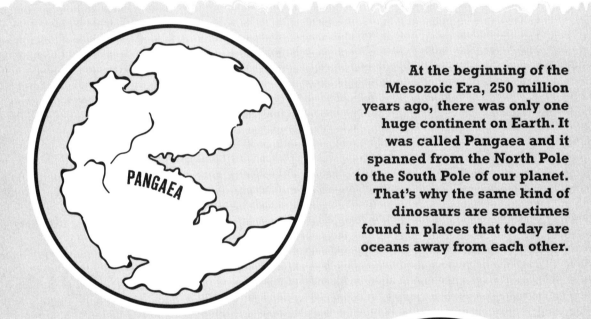

At the beginning of the Mesozoic Era, 250 million years ago, there was only one huge continent on Earth. It was called Pangaea and it spanned from the North Pole to the South Pole of our planet. That's why the same kind of dinosaurs are sometimes found in places that today are oceans away from each other.

Pangaea in the Triassic Period.

During the Jurassic Period, in the middle of the Mesozoic Era, Pangaea started splitting. The two new continents were called Gondwana and Laurasia.

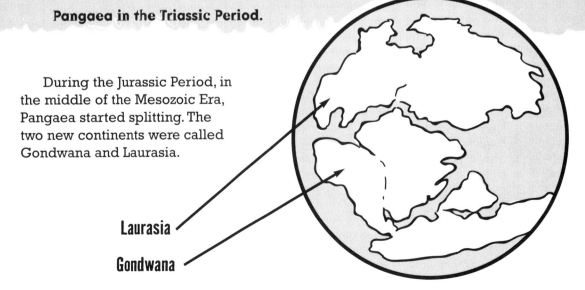

Laurasia

Gondwana

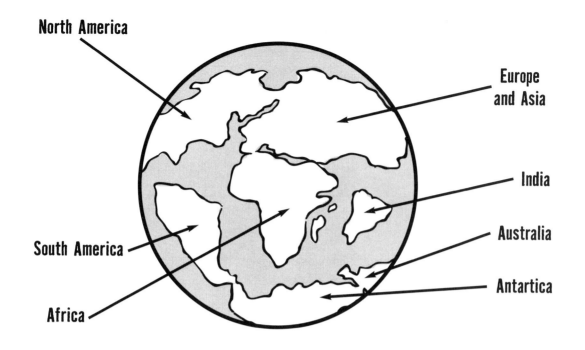

North America

Europe and Asia

India

Australia

Antartica

South America

Africa

By the time the Cretaceous Period ended, the Atlantic Ocean was still very narrow, while India wasn't part of Asia yet. Australia and Antarctica were still joined, but while Antarctica was moving toward the South Pole, Australia was getting closer to the position it's at today.

This is how our planet appears today. The continents are still drifting, continually changing the way Earth looks. They move at a rate of about one or two inches per year.

EUSTREPTOSPONDYLUS

yoo-strep-to-spon-dee-lus *"Well-Curved Vertebrae"*

FTEN MISTAKEN FOR **MEGALOSAURUS, EUSTREPTOSPONDYLUS,** ALTHOUGH MASSIVE, WAS A SMALL **EUROPEAN CARNOSAUR.**

SCALE

EUSTREPTOSPONDYLUS' DIMENSIONS ARE **APPROXIMATE,** SINCE A FULLY-GROWN SKELETON HAS NEVER BEEN **FOUND.**

TRIASSIC • JURASSIC • CRETACEOUS

WITH ITS **CLAWED HANDS** AND **SHARP TEETH**, **EUSTREPTOSPONDYLUS** WAS A **FEROCIOUS PREDATOR!**

ONLY **ONE SKELETON** OF A **YOUNG EUSTREPTOSPONDYLUS** HAS EVER BEEN FOUND.

PALEONTOLOGISTS KNOW IT MUST HAVE BEEN **YOUNG** BECAUSE THE **BONES** WERE NOT COMPLETELY **GROWN.**

LENGTH: 20 FEET
WEIGHT: 500 LBS

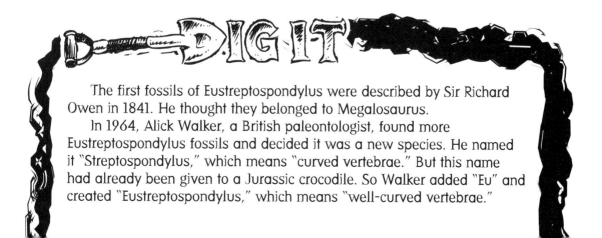

DIG IT

The first fossils of Eustreptospondylus were described by Sir Richard Owen in 1841. He thought they belonged to Megalosaurus.

In 1964, Alick Walker, a British paleontologist, found more Eustreptospondylus fossils and decided it was a new species. He named it "Streptospondylus," which means "curved vertebrae." But this name had already been given to a Jurassic crocodile. So Walker added "Eu" and created "Eustreptospondylus," which means "well-curved vertebrae."

LESOTHOSAURUS

le-so-tho-sawr-us *"Lizard from Lesotho"*

LESOTHOSAURUS WAS A **SMALL** DINOSAUR, THE SIZE OF AN **AVERAGE DOG!**

LENGTH: 3.5 FEET

SCALE

TRIASSIC • JURASSIC • CRETACEOUS

LESOTHOSAURUS WAS AN **ORNITHOPOD** (BIRD-FOOTED) DINOSAUR. IN FACT, ITS **FEET** LOOKED VERY MUCH LIKE THOSE OF A **CHICKEN.** IT HAD **FOUR TOES** WITH **CLAWS.** ONE **TOE** WAS VERY **TINY** AND WASN'T USED FOR **WALKING.**

LESOTHOSAURUS MUST HAVE BEEN A VERY **FAST RUNNER** BECAUSE ITS **BACK LEGS** AND **FEET** WERE **VERY LONG.**

DIG IT

Lesothosaurus was named by English paleontologist Peter Galton in 1978. The name means "Lizard from Lesotho," the African country where the first fossils were found. More Lesothosaurus fossils were later discovered in Venezuela.

THE
TRIASSIC PERIOD
(250 MYA - 206 MYA)

DURING THE **TRIASSIC PERIOD** THERE WAS ONLY ONE **SUPERCONTINENT** CALLED **PANGAEA**, WHICH IN GREEK MEANS **"ALL THE LANDS."** PANGAEA WAS SURROUNDED BY **PANTHALASSIA**, WHICH MEANS **"ALL THE SEAS."** AT THE CENTER OF PANGAEA WAS THE **SEA OF TETHYS**.

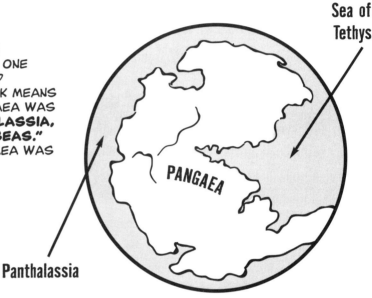

Sea of Tethys

PANGAEA

Panthalassia

THE WORD **TRIASSIC** WAS COINED BY GERMAN GEOLOGIST **FRIEDRICH AUGUST VON ALBERTI** IN 1834. HE NOTICED THAT IN GERMANY, ROCK FORMATIONS FROM THE **TRIASSIC PERIOD** WERE COMPOSED OF **THREE LAYERS**. HE CALLED THEM **TRIAS ("THREE")**, WHICH BECAME **TRIASSIC**.

GRASS AND **FLOWERS** HAD **NOT EVOLVED** YET. THE MOST **COMMON PLANTS** WERE **CYCADS, CONIFERS, HORSETAILS,** AND **FERNS**.

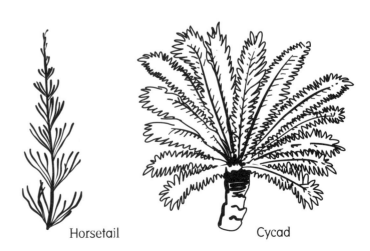

Horsetail

Cycad

IN THE SEA, ANIMALS LIKE **ICHTHYOSAURUS** (A DOLPHIN-LIKE REPTILE) WERE THRIVING. ON LAND, **TURTLES, FROGS, CROCODILES,** AND **LIZARDS** TOOK OVER.

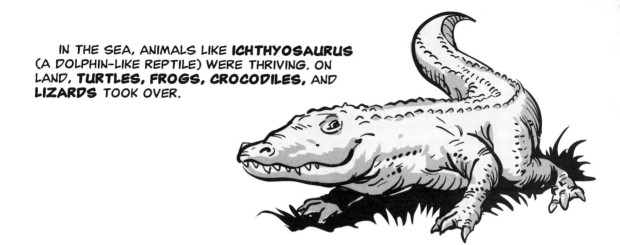

THE **CLIMATE** DURING THE TRIASSIC PERIOD WAS VERY **HOT** AND **DRY** AND THERE WERE NO **ICE CAPS** ON OUR PLANET.

Reptiles, like Eudimorphodon, were flying in the skys long before the birds.

Herrerasaurus was one of the first dinosaurs to appear.

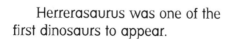

AT THE END OF THE TRIASSIC PERIOD A **MASS EXTINCTION** KILLED **40%** OF **LIFE.** MANY **NICHES** WERE **LEFT FREE.** BY FILLING THEM, THE **DINOSAURS** TOOK OVER THE **WORLD.**

THE JURASSIC PERIOD

(206 MYA - 144 MYA)

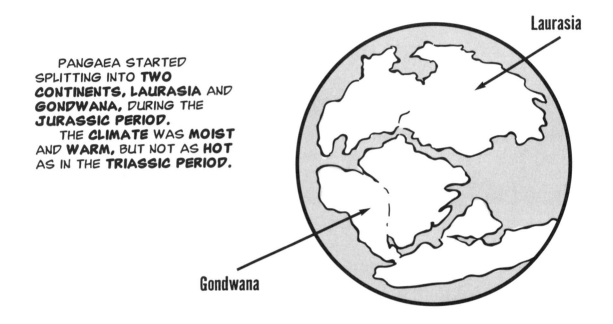

PANGAEA STARTED SPLITTING INTO **TWO CONTINENTS, LAURASIA** AND **GONDWANA,** DURING THE **JURASSIC PERIOD.**

THE **CLIMATE** WAS **MOIST** AND **WARM,** BUT NOT AS **HOT** AS IN THE **TRIASSIC PERIOD.**

Laurasia

Gondwana

IN 1795, **ALEXANDER VON HUMBOLT,** GERMAN NATURALIST AND EXPLORER, STUDIED A **LAYER** OF **ROCKS** IN THE **JURA MOUNTAINS,** LOCATED BETWEEN **FRANCE** AND **SWITZERLAND.** THIS LAYER OF ROCKS HAD FORMED ABOUT **200 MILLION YEARS AGO,** DURING A LONG SPAN OF TIME. VON HUMBOLT CALLED IT **JURASSIC PERIOD,** AFTER THE **JURA MOUNTAINS.**

FROM THE **CYCADS,** PLANTS CALLED **BENNETTITALES** EVOLVED. THEY WERE THE **ANCESTORS** OF THE MODERN **FLOWERING PLANTS.**

Bennettitales

Ferocious Allosaurus was terrifying its victims.

Pterodactylus flew in the skies.

Apatosaurus was one of the biggest animals ever to walk on land.

Mammals, from which we descend, had already evolved. They remained small and were possibly nocturnal.

THE CRETACEOUS PERIOD

(144 MYA – 65 MYA)

DURING MOST OF THE **CRETACEOUS PERIOD,** THE **CLIMATE** WAS STILL **WARM** AND **MOIST,** MUCH LIKE THE **JURASSIC PERIOD.**

GONDWANA AND **LAURASIA** WERE **SPLITTING** APART, FORMING THE **CONTINENTS** AS WE KNOW THEM TODAY.

BELGIAN GEOLOGIST **JEAN-BAPTISTE-JULIEN D'OMALIUS D'HALLOY** DISCOVERED A **CHALKY LAYER** OF **ROCKS,** WHICH WERE **FORMED** DURING THE **CRETACEOUS PERIOD.** THE WORD **CRETACEOUS** COMES FROM THE LATIN "CRETA" WHICH MEANS **CHALK.**

FLOWERING PLANTS, LIKE **MAGNOLIAS, BIRCHES,** AND **WILLOWS** APPEARED ON **EARTH** FOR THE **FIRST TIME.**

Magnolia

NEW **DINOSAUR SPECIES** TOOK OVER WHILE OTHERS
BECAME EXTINCT. **T. REX, DUCK-BILLED,** AND **HORNED
DINOSAURS** EVOLVED.

Centrosaurus and
T. rex lived at the same
time in North America.

AS THE **FLOWERING PLANTS** SPREAD, NEW SPECIES OF
INSECTS EVOLVED: **BUTTERFLIES, ANTS,** AND **BEES!**

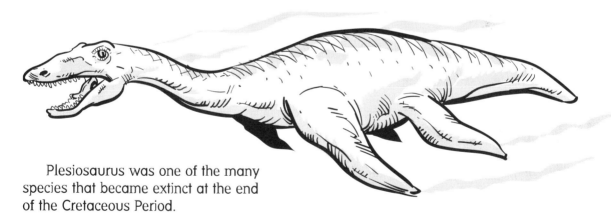

Plesiosaurus was one of the many
species that became extinct at the end
of the Cretaceous Period.

THE **END** OF THE **CRETACEOUS PERIOD** WAS MARKED BY A HUGE **MASS
EXTINCTION** THAT **KILLED** ALL THE **DINOSAURS, FLYING REPTILES, MARINE
REPTILES,** SEVERAL **PLANTS** AND OTHER **ANIMALS.** AMONG THE **SURVIVORS**
THERE WERE **MAMMALS** AND **BIRDS.**

KENTROSAURUS

ken-troh-sawr-us "Spike Lizard"

KENTROSAURUS WASN'T VERY **SMART.** LIKE **STEGOSAURUS,** KENTROSAURUS' **BODY** WAS **BIG,** BUT ITS **BRAIN** WAS JUST ABOUT THE SIZE OF A **WALNUT!**

KENTROSAURUS OWES ITS NAME TO THE MANY **SPIKES** RUNNING ALONG PART OF ITS **BACK** ALL THE WAY DOWN TO ITS **TAIL. "KENTRON"** MEANS "SPIKE" IN GREEK.

KENTROSAURUS' **SPIKES** WERE USED FOR **SELF-DEFENSE.** BY SWINGING ITS **TAIL,** KENTROSAURUS COULD **BADLY INJURE** ITS **ATTACKER.**

LENGTH: 15 FEET WEIGHT: 2 TONS

TRIASSIC   JURASSIC   CRETACEOUS

Kentrosaurus' back legs were longer than its front legs, so its head was very close to the ground. This arrangement helped Kentrosaurus graze on small plants.

KENTROSAURUS' SPIKES COULD BE UP TO **TWO FEET LONG!**

SCALE

ENTROSAURUS ALSO HAD **TWO SPIKES** ON ITS **FLANKS.** THESE MUST HAVE MADE **KENTROSAURUS** A DANGEROUS PREY TO **BITE!**

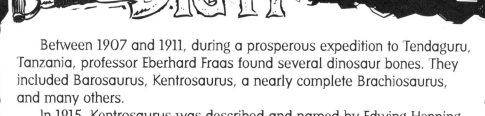

DIG IT

Between 1907 and 1911, during a prosperous expedition to Tendaguru, Tanzania, professor Eberhard Fraas found several dinosaur bones. They included Barosaurus, Kentrosaurus, a nearly complete Brachiosaurus, and many others.

In 1915, Kentrosaurus was described and named by Edwing Henning, one of the paleontologists who participated in the fruitful expedition.

CETIOSAURUS

e-o-sawr-us "*Whale-like Lizard*"

CETIOSAURUS WAS ONE OF THE FIRST **SAUROPODS,** A GROUP INCLUDING ENORMOUS **BAROSAURUS** AND **APATOSAURUS.** CETIOSAURUS WASN'T AS **BIG** AS THEM, BUT IT WAS STILL PRETTY **MASSIVE.**

TRIASSIC ● JURASSIC ● CRETACEOUS

SCALE

A **THIGHBONE** OF **CETIOSAURUS** UNEARTHED IN 1979 IN **MOROCCO** WAS OVER SIX FEET LONG, TALLER THAN AN **AVERAGE PERSON!**

ITS **STIFF TAIL** WAS PROBABLY KEPT **PARALLEL** TO THE **GROUND** TO COUNTERBALANCE THE **WEIGHT** OF ITS **NECK.**

Footnote: Cetiosaurus' fossils have been found only in England and Morocco.

DIG IT

Cetiosaurus was described by Sir Richard Owen in 1841. He didn't named it "Whale-Like Lizard" because of the massive bulk of this dinosaur. But because Owen had noticed some similarities between the shape of Cetiosaurus' back bones and those of whales.

ANCHISAURUS

ank-eeh-sawr-us   *"Near Lizard"*

ANCHISAURUS WALKED ON ALL **FOUR LEGS** MOST OF THE TIME, BUT IT PROBABLY **DASHED AWAY** FROM **PREDATORS** BY RUNNING ONLY ON ITS **TWO LONG BACK LEGS!**

← SCALE →

●   **TRIASSIC**   ●   **JURASSIC**   ●   **CRETACEOUS**

WHEN IT WAS DOWN ON ALL FOURS, **ANCHISAURUS** COULD EAT **LOW VEGETATION** AND **ROOTS,** WHICH IT **UNEARTHED** WITH THE **AID** OF ITS **CLAW.**

ANCHISAURUS' CLAW WAS ALSO USED FOR **SELF-DEFENSE** AGAINST PREDATORS.

ANCHISAURUS HAD **FIVE FINGERS,** BUT **TWO** WERE **VERY SMALL.**

LENGTH: 7 FEET
WEIGHT: 70 LBS

Footnote: Fossils of Anchisaurus have been found in Connecticut Valley and southern Africa. This indicates once more that at one time all the lands were joined together forming a super-continent, Pangaea.

DIG IT

Anchisaurus was described in 1885 by American paleontologist Othniel Marsh.

TYRANNOSAURUS YUKs!

7. WHAT **DINOSAUR** MAKES A LOT OF **NOISE** WHEN IT **SLEEPS?**

—STEGA-**SNORE**-US!

8. WHAT'S THE **BEST WAY** TO TALK TO AN **ALLOSAURUS?**

—LONG DISTANCE!

9. WHERE DOES A **MAMENCHISARUS** BUY ITS **CLOTHES?**

—AT THE DINO-**STORE!**

10. WHICH **DINOSAUR** IS MOST LIKE A **LEAKY FAUCET?**

—**DRYPT**-O-SAURUS!

11. WHICH **DINOSAUR** TAKES THE **BEST PHOTOGRAPHS?**

—**CAMARA**-SAURUS!

12. WHICH **DINOSAUR** CAN YOU **EAT OFF** OF?

—**PLATE**-O-SAURUS!

ORNITHOLESTES

or-nith-oh-les-teez "Bird Thief"

RNITHOLESTES' BODY WAS VERY **SLIM** AND ITS **LEGS** WERE VERY **LONG.** THESE TRAITS INDICATE ORNITHOLESTES WAS VERY **AGILE** AND COULD **RUN** EXTREMELY **FAST.** SOME RESEARCHERS THINK ORNITHOLESTES WAS SO FAST IT **HUNTED BIRDS.** SO ITS **NAME** MEANS **"BIRD THIEF."**

LENGTH: 6.5 FEET
WEIGHT: 30 LBS

DIG IT

Ornitholestes was named by legendary dinosaur hunter Henry Fairfield Osborn in 1903.

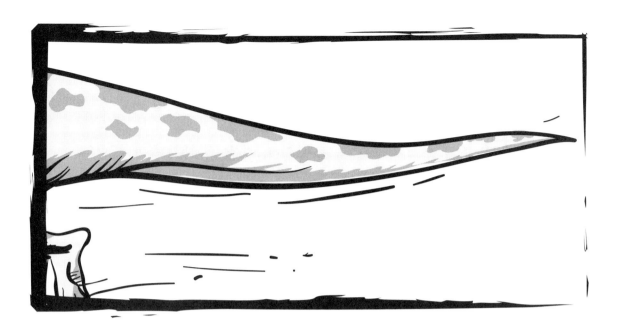

ORNITHOLESTES WAS ONE OF THE **SMALLEST DINOSAURS** AND ITS **STIFF TAIL** ACCOUNTED FOR MORE THAN **HALF** ITS **TOTAL LENGTH.** ORNITHOLESTES USED ITS **TAIL** TO **COUNTERBALANCE** ITS **BODY WEIGHT** WHEN IT MADE **SHARP TURNS** WHILE RUNNING.

THE **FUNCTION** OF THE **BUMP** ON **ORNITHOLESTES' NOSE** REMAINS A **MYSTERY.**

SCALE

ORNITHOLESTES MIGHT HAVE ALSO **HUNTED** AND **EATEN** LITTLE **REPTILES** AND **RODENTS.**

TRIASSIC   JURASSIC   CRETACEOUS

DILOPHOSAURUS

dye-loh-foo-sawr-us   *"Double-crested Lizard"*

DILOPHOSAURUS HAD **SHORT ARMS** AND **HANDS** WITH ONLY **THREE FINGERS**. ITS FEET HAD **FOUR TOES**, BUT ONE WAS A **DEWCLAW** (A **CLAW** THAT DID NOT REACH THE **GROUND**).

● TRIASSIC ● JURASSIC ● CRETACEOUS

ON TOP OF **DILOPHOSAURUS' HEAD** WERE **TWO CRESTS** MADE OF **BONE.** NOBODY KNOWS WHAT THEY WERE USED FOR. ONE **THEORY** IS THAT THEY REVEALED DILOPHOSAURUS' **GENDER:** A **MALE** MIGHT HAVE HAD TWO **BIG** CRESTS, A **FEMALE** TWO **SMALL** ONES, AND A **YOUNG** DILOPHOSAURUS PROBABLY HAD **NO CRESTS** AT ALL.

DILOPHOSAURUS WAS A **CARNIVORE.** ITS **TEETH** WERE **SHARP,** BUT **WEAK.** TO KILL ITS **PREY, DILOPHOSAURUS** USED ITS **FOOT CLAWS!**

LENGTH: 20 FEET
HEIGHT: 5 FEET
WEIGHT: 700 LBS

Footnote: The stride length of a Dilophosaurus was about five feet.

DROMAEOSAURUS

droh-mee-o-sawr-us "*Running Lizard*"

DROMAEOSAURUS WAS A VERY **FAST** AND **VICIOUS PREDATOR.** IT HAD A **LARGE BRAIN** AND WAS **VERY INTELLIGENT.** DROMAEOSAURUS WAS PROBABLY ABLE TO **HUNT** IN **PACKS.**

DIG IT

Dromaeosaurus was the first dinosaur of its kind to be discovered. The Dromaeosaur family takes its name after this dinosaur.

Dromaeosaurus fossils were found in 1915 in Alberta, Canada, by Barnum Brown, who also named this dinosaur.

ITS **CURVED TEETH** WERE MADE FOR **SHREDDING MEAT.** DROMAEOSAURUS WAS **CARNIVOROUS.**

DROMAEOSAURUS' HANDS WERE ABLE TO **GRAB** ITS **VICTIM,** AND HOLD IT **STILL** FOR THE **KILLING.**

DROMAEOSAURUS HAD A **SICKLE-LIKE CLAW** ON EACH **FOOT.** WITH THIS **WEAPON, DROMAEOSAURUS** FINISHED OFF ITS **PREY.**

SCALE

LENGTH:
6 FEET
WEIGHT:
30 LBS

TRIASSIC   JURASSIC   CRETACEOUS

VELOCIRAPTOR

veh-loh-see-rap-tor "Swift Thief"

VELOCIRAPTOR'S MOST POWERFUL **WEAPONS** WERE THE **SEVEN-INCH-LONG SICKLE-LIKE CLAWS** AT THE END OF ITS **TOES.** VELOCIRAPTOR HAD TO KEEP THEM **RAISED** FROM THE GROUND WHEN IT **WALKED.** BUT WHEN IT ATTACKED ITS **PREY,** IT TURNED THEM DOWN TO SLASH ITS **VICTIM!**

V

VELOCIRAPTOR WAS A SMALL, **AGILE,** AND **FAST** DINOSAUR. IT COULD **RUN** UP TO **40 MILES PER HOUR!**

VELOCIRAPTOR HAD A **VERY LARGE BRAIN** COMPARED TO ITS **BODY SIZE.** THIS MEANS IT WAS VERY **INTELLIGENT. CARNIVORES** LIKE **VELOCIRAPTOR** ARE GENERALLY **MORE INTELLIGENT** THAN **HERBIVORES.**

Velociraptor was first found by American Museum of Natural History paleontologist Henry Fairfield Osborn, in 1924 in Mongolia.

VELOCIRAPTOR

WEIGHT: 30 LBS

HEIGHT: 3 FEET

LENGTH: 6 FEET

SCALE

VELOCIRAPTOR HAD CLAWS AT THE END OF ITS FINGERS. IT MUST HAVE BEEN VERY HARD FOR ITS VICTIMS TO GET THEMSELVES FREE FROM VELOCIRAPTOR'S GRASP!

SOME **MICRORAPTOR** FOSSILS BEAR **MARKS** INDICATING THAT THIS DINOSAUR HAD **FEATHERS.** SINCE **MICRORAPTOR** AND **VELOCIRAPTOR** BELONGED TO THE SAME **FAMILY,** IT'S POSSIBLE THAT **VELOCIRAPTOR** MIGHT ALSO HAVE HAD **FEATHERS.**

T HE **FOSSILS** OF SOME **YOUNG VELOCIRAPTORS** WERE FOUND IN AN **OVIRAPTOR'S NEST.** THE **YOUNG VELOCIRAPTORS** COULD HAVE BEEN THERE TO **STEAL** OVIRAPTOR'S **EGGS.**

OR MAYBE THEY WERE OVIRAPTOR'S **DINNER!** OVIRAPTOR COULD HAVE **HUNTED** THEM AND BROUGHT THEM BACK TO ITS **NEST** TO FEED ITS **BABIES!**

IN EITHER CASE, THEY WERE SURPRISED BY A **SAND STORM** THAT **KILLED** THEM AND QUICKLY **BURIED** THEM. AND THAT'S HOW THEY **FOSSILIZED** AND WERE **PRESERVED** UNTIL TODAY.

FOSSILIZATION

Fossilization is the gradual replacement of bones by minerals, and it takes millions of years to complete. There's really no bone left in a fossilized dinosaur skeleton! This is how it works...

A dinosaur dies by a river and the debris brought by the water quickly buries it. Animals that are not buried quickly are often eaten by scavengers or just disintegrate in time.

Time goes by and the deposits continue to pile up on the dinosaur's carcass. In the meantime, soft tissues like skin and internal organs disperse. The bones are very slowly replaced by minerals.

With the passage of the millennia, the river might dry up, an earthquake might occur, or the climate might become hot and dry. All these changes modify the landscape, and the fossilized bones now come to the surface.

Paleontologists are very careful in digging up a fossilized dinosaur. They want to make sure that no bones are lost in the excavating process. Some researchers take pictures of the findings, while others measure them. Eventually the fossilized dinosaur is retrieved and can be displayed in a museum!

TRICERATOPS

try-see-rah-tops   *"Three-Horned Face"*

TRICERATOPS WAS A VERY **COMMON** DINOSAUR OF THE END OF THE **CRETACEOUS PERIOD.** IT LIVED IN **HERDS** AND **MIGRATED** IN SEARCH OF **FOOD.**

ALL DINOSAURS LAID **EGGS,** BUT UNLIKE MANY OF THEM, **TRICERATOPS** MIGHT HAVE TAKEN CARE OF ITS **YOUNG.**

TRICERATOPS WAS NAMED AFTER THE **THREE HORNS** ON ITS **FACE.** THE **TWO** OVER ITS **EYES** COULD REACH **THREE FEET IN LENGTH!** THE ONE ON ITS **NOSE** WAS MUCH SMALLER.

PALEONTOLOGISTS HAVE NOTICED **HEALED SCARS** ON THE **FOSSILS** OF MANY **TRICETOPS' SKULLS.** THEY CONCLUDED **TRICERATOPS** ENGAGED IN **FIGHTS** WITH THE OTHER MEMBERS OF ITS **HERD.** THESE **FIGHTS** COULD BE **VIOLENT,** BUT PROBOBLY **NOT DEADLY. TRICERATOPS** MIGHT HAVE FOUGHT DURING **MATING SEASON** OR TO ESTABLISH **LEADERSHIP.**

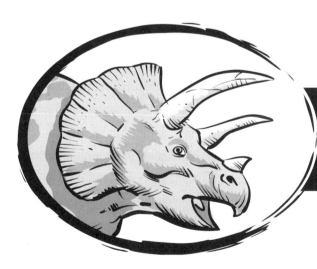

TRICERATOPS' MOUTH HAD A **STRONG BEAK** AND **SHARP TEETH** TO CHEW **VEGETATION** AND **ROOTS.**

DIG IT

While analyzing the first Triceratops fossils ever discovered, Othniel Marsh thought the horns belonged to an extinct species of buffalo.

Later on, when more fossils were found, Marsh realized that it was a new species of dinosaur.

TRICERATOPS

TRICERATOPS WAS ONE OF THE **LAST** DINOSAURS TO BECOME **EXTINCT.**

TRICERATOPS PROTECTED ITS **HERD** WHEN ASSAILED BY A **PREDATOR.** THIS **TEN TON** ANIMAL WOULD CHARGE **HEAD DOWN,** LIKE A MODERN **RHINO,** TRYING TO **STAB** ITS **ENEMY** WITH ITS **POWERFUL HORNS!**

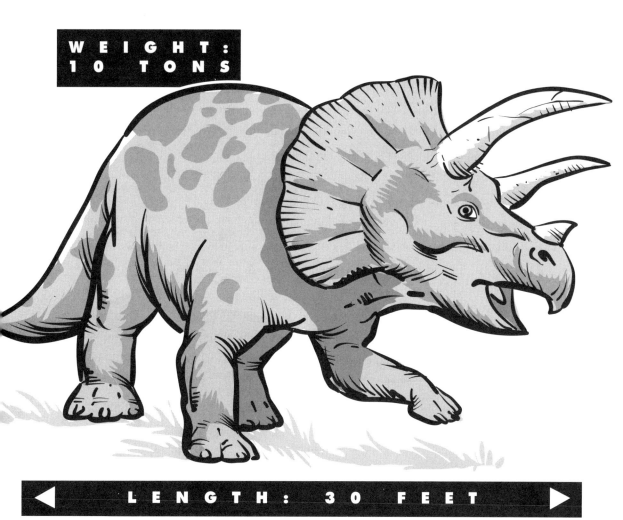

ITS **SKULL** WAS **HUGE**: IT MEASURED **SIX FEET** FROM ITS **MOUTH** TO THE END OF ITS **FRILL**.

WEIGHT: 10 TONS

◄ **LENGTH: 30 FEET** ►

SCALE

TRICERATOPS FOSSILS HAVE BEEN FOUND IN **WYOMING, MONTANA,** AND **SOUTH DAKOTA,** AS WELL AS IN **ALBERTA, CANADA.**

Footnote: Triceratops was one of the biggest Ceratopsian (horned-nosed dinosaurs). This group includes Torosaurus and Centrosaurus.

SPINOSAURUS

spy-no-sawr-us   *"Spiny Lizard"*

SPINOSAURUS WAS PROBABLY A **PISCIVORE,** OR **FISH-EATER,** BECAUSE ITS **TEETH** RESEMBLE THOSE OF MODERN FISH-EATING REPTILES.

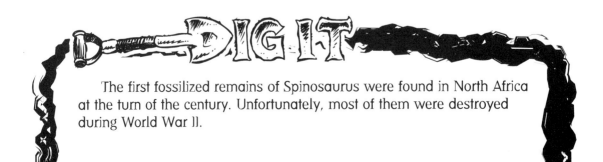

The first fossilized remains of Spinosaurus were found in North Africa at the turn of the century. Unfortunately, most of them were destroyed during World War II.

SPINOSAURUS' MOST IMPRESSIVE FEATURE WAS THE **SAIL** ON ITS **BACK**. THE SAIL WAS MADE OF **SPIKES** UP TO **SIX FEET** LONG. SOME SCIENTISTS BELIEVE THAT **SPINOSAURUS' SAIL** WAS VERY **COLORFUL** AND WAS USED TO ATTRACT **MATES**.

ANOTHER **THEORY** IS BASED ON THE BELIEF THAT DINOSAURS WERE **COLD-BLOODED**. JUST LIKE **STEGOSAURUS** USED ITS **PLATES** TO REGULATE ITS **INTERNAL TEMPERATURE**, SPINOSAURUS USED ITS **SAIL**.

WHEN THE **SAIL** WAS TURNED TOWARD THE **SUN**, THE **BLOOD** CIRCULATING THROUGH IT BECAME **WARMER**. THEN, RUNNING THROUGH SPINOSAURUS' **BODY**, THE BLOOD WOULD **WARM UP** THE **WHOLE ANIMAL**. IN THE SAME WAY, BY TURNING THE SAIL **AWAY** FROM THE **SUN**, SPINOSAURUS **COOLED DOWN**.

```
LENGTH:
40  FEET
WEIGHT:
4  TONS
```

SCALE

Footnote: Spinosaurus' arms and hands were much bigger than other meat-eating dinosaurs. So, although it was bipedal, Spinosaurus might have also walked on both its hands and feet some of the time.

TRIASSIC ● JURASSIC ● CRETACEOUS

OVIRAPTOR

oh-vi-rap-tor "Egg Thief"

OVIRAPTOR WAS AN **OMNIVORE** WITH A POWERFUL **JAW** AND **NO TEETH**—ONLY A STRONG **BEAK**.

ITS **HANDS** WERE ABLE TO **GRASP** THINGS.

ITS **CLAWS** COULD REACH **THREE INCHES** IN LENGTH.

OVIRAPTOR HAD A SMALL **CREST** ON ITS **NOSE,** BUT PALEONTOLOGISTS DON'T KNOW EXACTLY WHAT IT WAS **USED** FOR. MAYBE IT WAS JUST TO **SHOW OFF** AN OVIRAPTOR'S **RANK** AND **GENDER.**

SCALE

LENGTH: 6 FEET

TRIASSIC • JURASSIC • CRETACEOUS

IN 1924, **OVIRAPTOR** WAS FIRST DISCOVERED IN **MONGOLIA**, DURING AN **EXPEDITION** FOR THE **AMERICAN MUSEUM OF NATURAL HISTORY.** OVIRAPTOR'S **FOSSILS** WERE FOUND ON A **NEST** THAT WAS THOUGHT TO BELONG TO A **PROTOCERATOPS.**

SCIENTISTS CONCLUDED **OVIRAPTOR** FED ON **EGGS** IT STOLE FROM OTHER DINOSAURS' **NESTS,** AND NAMED IT "**EGG THIEF.**"

A MORE RECENT EXPEDITION UNEARTHED ANOTHER **OVIRAPTOR** ALSO SITTING ON A **NEST** CONTAINING **EGGS.** BUT INSIDE THESE **EGGS,** RESEARCHERS FOUND **BABY OVIRAPTORS.**

THIS **DISCOVERY** PROVED OVIRAPTOR WASN'T AN EGG THIEF, BUT PROBABLY A CARING PARENT TRYING TO HATCH ITS BABIES. ALSO, THE **NEST** ORIGINALLY THOUGHT TO BELONG TO **PROTOCERATOPS** WAS ACTUALLY **OVIRAPTOR'S.**

SAUROLOPHUS

sawr-ol-oh-fus   *"Crested Lizard"*

WEIGHT: 3 TONS

HEIGHT: 15 FEET

LENGTH: 30 FEET

SAUROLOPHUS' HEAD WAS ADORNED WITH A **FIVE-INCH-LONG HORN.** SOME PALEONTOLOGISTS THINK **SAUROLOPHUS** WAS ABLE TO INFLATE THE **SKIN** COVERING ITS **CREST** AND **NOSE** TO MAKE **LOUD SOUNDS.**

SCALE

TRIASSIC   JURASSIC   CRETACEOUS

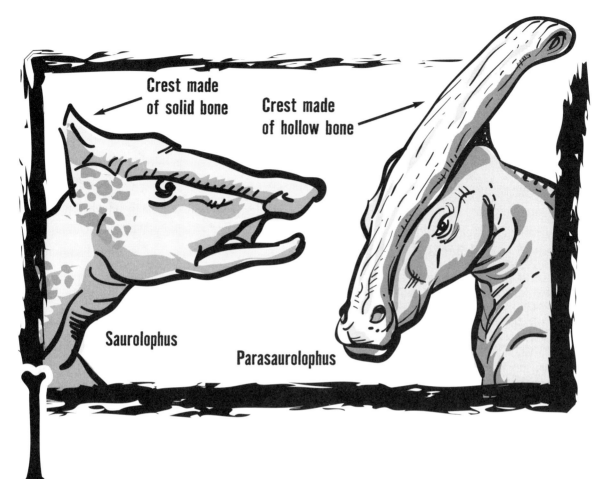

Crest made of solid bone

Crest made of hollow bone

Saurolophus

Parasaurolophus

I N 1922, TEN YEARS AFTER THE DISCOVERY OF **SAUROLOPHUS,** CANADIAN PALEONTOLOGIST **WILLIAM PARKS** FOUND THE **FIRST FOSSILS** OF ANOTHER **CRESTED DINOSAUR.**

PARKS DECIDED TO NAME THE NEW DISCOVERY **PARASAUROLOPHUS,** WHICH MEANS **"SIMILAR TO SAUROLOPHUS."** PARKS' CHOICE WAS BASED ON THE FACT THAT PARASAUROLOPHUS' CREST **CLOSELY RESEMBLED** TO THE ONE ON SAUROLOPHUS' **HEAD.**

BOTH DINOSAURS BELONGED TO THE **DUCK-BILLED FAMILY,** CHARACTERIZED BY A **TOOTHLESS FLAT SNOUT,** VERY MUCH LIKE A **DUCK'S BEAK.** BUT WE KNOW TODAY THAT THEY WERE **VERY DIFFERENT** FROM EACH OTHER.

SAUROLOPHUS BELONGS TO A GROUP OF DUCK-BILLED DINOSAURS CALLED **HADROSAURINE.** THEIR **CRESTS** WERE **SOLID** AND **BONY.**

PARASAUROLOPHUS BELONGS TO A GROUP OF DUCK-BILLED DINOSAURS CALLED **LAMBEOSAURINE,** BEARING **HUGE, HOLLOW CRESTS.**

Saurolophus' first fossils were found in Canada by Barnum Brown in 1912, who also named this dinosaur. Since then more fossils have been found in Mongolia.

PARASAUROLOPHUS

par-us-sawr-ol-oh-fus   *"Similar to Saurolophus"*

PARASAUROLOPHUS' CREST COULD BE UP TO **SEVEN FEET LONG!** IT WAS MADE OF **HOLLOW BONE** AND CONNECTED TO PARASAUROLOPHUS' **NOSTRILS.**

PALEONTOLOGISTS THINK PARASAUROLOPHUS LIVED IN **HERDS** AND USED ITS **CREST** TO MAKE **SOUNDS.**

SOUNDS ARE **VERY IMPORTANT** FOR A HERD. FOR EXAMPLE, **CALLING SOUNDS** KEEP THE **HERD TOGETHER,** AND **WARNING SOUNDS** ALERT THE OTHERS OF **IMPENDING DANGER.**

DIG IT

Like all the duck-billed dinosaurs, Parasaurolophus had a toothless beak. It also had a battery of powerful cheek teeth that were able to chew the toughest vegetation.

PARASAUROLOPHUS HAD A **NOTCH** ON ITS **SPINE** WHERE ITS CREST **RESTED.**

AN **OLD THEORY** SUGGESTS THAT PARASAUROLOPHUS' LIVED IN **WATER** AND WAS A **GOOD SWIMMER.** IT HAD **WEBBED FEET,** A **THICK TAIL** THAT ENABLED IT TO **SWIM,** AND USED ITS **CREST** LIKE A **SNORKEL** WHEN IT DOVE **UNDERWATER.**

THE THEORY WAS LATER **ABANDONED.** ALTHOUGH PARASAUROLOPHUS MIGHT HAVE LIVED **NEAR WATER,** IT'S UNLIKELY IT LIVED UNDER IT BECAUSE NO **NOSTRIL OPENINGS** WERE EVER FOUND ON TOP OF ITS **CREST.**

SCALE

TRIASSIC ● JURASSIC ● CRETACEOUS

ALBERTA, CANADA: **68 MILLION YEARS AGO.** A HERD OF **PARASAUROLOPHUSES** IS GRAZING, UNAWARE OF THE **LOOMING DANGER...**

...A **PREDATOR** HAS PICKED UP THEIR **SCENT!**

THE PREDATOR IS NONE OTHER THAN A VICIOUS AND HUNGRY T. REX!
SUDDENLY T. REX ATTACKS THE HERD!
RRRAAWWWRRR
UUURRR!

STARTLED, **T. REX** TURNS, RELEASING ITS **CATCH!**
WWWIIEERRAAWWW
WWWIIEERRAAWWW
THE **HERD** ESCAPES, **SCREECHING** AS THEY GO!

CENTROSAURUS

sen-tro-sawr-us   *"Sharp-Pointed Frill Lizard"*

DURING THE CRETACEOUS PERIOD, **CENTROSAURUS HERDS** ROAMED IN **NORTH AMERICA.** THEY MIGRATED FROM **PLACE** TO **PLACE,** SEARCHING FOR NEW **SOURCES** OF **FOOD.**

DURING ONE OF THESE MIGRATIONS, A **HERD** WAS OVERTAKEN BY A **RIVER FLOOD.** THE **STARTLED ANIMALS** TRAMPLED EACH OTHER AND EVENTUALLY THEY ALL **DROWNED.**

IN 1978, IN ALBERTA, CANADA, PALEONTOLOGIST **PHILIP CURRIE** FOUND THE **FOSSILIZED HERD.**

SINCE THEIR DEATH, THE RIVER HAD **DISAPPEARED,** BUT THE HERD'S **BONE BED** WAS STILL **PRESERVED.**

TRIASSIC   JURASSIC   CRETACEOUS

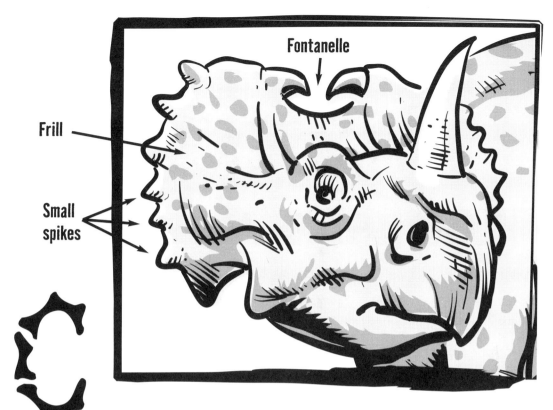

Fontanelle

Frill

Small spikes

C

ENTROSAURUS' FRILL WAS SHORT AND ADORNED WITH SMALL SPIKES. ON TOP OF THE FRILL, THERE WAS A FONTANELLE, OR OPENING, WITH TWO SPIKES POINTING IN.

ITS STURDY FRILL MADE IT IMPOSSIBLE FOR PREDATORS TO BITE CENTROSAURUS' NECK, ONE OF THE MOST VULNERABLE PARTS OF THE BODY.

BESIDES ITS STURDY FRILL, CENTROSAURUS' SELF-DEFENSE WEAPON WAS A LONG HORN ON ITS NOSE. IF ATTACKED, CENTROSAURUS CHARGED ITS PREDATORS HEAD DOWN, TRYING TO THROW THEM OFF BALANCE. THEN, CENTROSAURUS STAB THEM.

LENGTH: 20 FEET
WEIGHT: 2 TONS

DIG IT

Centrosaurus was first described and named by Canadian paleontologist Lawrence Lambe in 1914.

UNSOLVED
MYSTERIES
"MOKELE-MBEMBE"

Although extinct for millions of years, prehistoric animals
seem to reappear in the most unlikely places!

EYE WITNESSES DESCRIBE **MOKELE-MBEMBE** AS A **HUGE APATOSAURUS**
WITH A **LONG NECK** AND **TAIL**. DESPITE **APATOSAURUS'** COMPLETE EXTINCTION
150 MILLION YEARS AGO, SOME PEOPLE STILL BELIEVE THAT THERE'S A **HERD OF
THEM** LIVING AT **LAKE TELE**, IN A **SWAMP REGION** OF THE **PEOPLE'S REPUBLIC
OF CONGO**, AFRICA.

IN 1913, **CAPT. FREIHERR VON STEIN ZU LAUSNITZ,** A GERMAN EXPLORER, COLLECTED **EYEWITNESS REPORTS** FROM THE **PYGMY,** THE **NATIVE PEOPLE** OF CONGO. HIS **REPORT** SPARKED MANY **EXPEDITIONS** TO **LAKE TELE.**

MANY OF THOSE WHO WENT TO THE **LAKE** CLAIMED TO HAVE SEEN **MOKELE-MBEMBE,** BUT NO ONE WAS EVER ABLE TO BRING BACK **IRREFUTABLE PROOF** OF THE **MONSTER'S EXISTENCE.**

MOKELE-MBEMBE MEANS **"THE ONE STOPPING THE RIVERS,"** AN APT NAME FOR SUCH AN **ENORMOUS BEAST!**

CAPT. FREIHERR VON STEIN ZU LAUSNITZ RECOUNTS THAT ONCE SOME **PYGMIES** WERE ABLE TO **CATCH** AND **KILL** A MOKELE-MBEBE. THEY **COOKED** IT AND **ATE** IT, BUT THEY EVENTUALLY ALL **DIED** OF **FOOD POISONING!**

NODOSAURUS

no-do-sawr-us   *"Knobby Lizard"*

NODOSAURUS' BACK WAS COVERED BY ROWS OF PLATES. IN EACH PLATE THERE WAS A BONY BUMP OR "KNOB." NODOSAURUS' NAME MEANS, IN FACT, "KNOBBY LIZARD."

SCALE

ONE OF THE MANY **"ARMORED DINOSAURS,"** ITS **SHORT LEGS** AND **LUMBERING BODY** MADE IT IMPOSSIBLE FOR **NODOSAURUS** TO **RUN AWAY** FROM **PREDATORS.** SO NODOSAURUS RELIED ON ITS **BONY SHIELD** FOR **PROTECTION.**

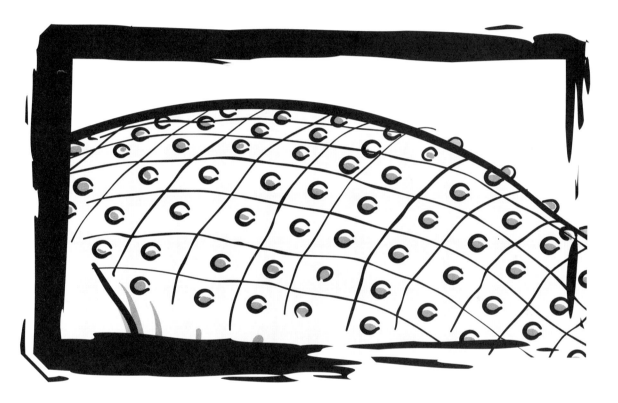

ITS **TEETH** WEREN'T VERY **STRONG,** SO NODOSAURUS COULD ONLY EAT **SOFT VEGETATION.**

LENGTH: 20 FEET

DIG IT

Nodosaurus was first described by American paleontologist Othniel Marsh in 1889.

CELEBRITY-SAURUS

STEVEN SPIELBERG-OSAURUS

When movie director Steven Spielberg donated funds for the research on dinosaurs in China, paleontologists thanked him by allowing him to name a specimen of Tianchisaurus. This dinosaur was first found near the Chinese lake of Tian Chi (Heaven Lake), from which it gets its name.

Spielberg came up with **Jurassosaurus nedegoapeferima**. The first part of this complicated name refers to **JURASSIC PARK**, Spielberg's movie about dinosaurs. The second part is made up of the two initial letters of the names of the main actors in the movie: Sam **Ne**ill, Laura **De**rn, Jeff **Go**ldblum, Richard **At**tenborough, Bob **Pe**ck, Martin **Fe**rrero, Ariana **Ri**chards, and Joseph **Ma**zzello.

★ CELEBRITY-SAURUS

DINOS, FOSSILS, AND ROCK N' ROLL!

Masiakasaurus was a piscivore with the most unusual teeth.

During a recent expedition, paleontologist **Scott Sampson** of the University of Utah unearthed a brand new dinosaur. The specimen was named **Masiakasaurus knopfleri.**

"**Masiaka**" means "vicious" in the native language of Madagascar, Africa, where the fossils were discovered. "**Knopfleri**" honors **Mark Knopfler**, the leader of the rock group **Dire Straits.** The paleontologists believe **Mark Knopfler's music** brought them **luck** during the escavations that unearthed the incredible discovery.

STYRACOSAURUS

sty-rak-uh-sawr-us   *"Spiked Lizard"*

LIKE MOST **CERATOPSIANS** (HORNED DINOSAURS LIKE **TRICERATOPS**) STYRACOSAURUS LIVED IN HERDS. HERDS PROVIDE PROTECTION FOR **VEGETARIAN** ANIMALS. A GROUP OF MANY CAN BE ABLE TO **SCARE AWAY** EVEN THE **FIERCEST PREDATOR.**

SCALE

TRIASSIC   JURASSIC   CRETACEOUS

This dinosaur could RUN! In spite of its massive body, Styracosaurs could reach the speed of 20 miles per hour!

STYRACOSAURUS' NOSE HORN WAS **TWO FEET LONG** AND **SIX INCHES WIDE!**

STYRACOSAURUS' FRILL WASN'T ALL MADE OF **BONE.** THERE WERE TWO **BIG "WINDOWS"** COVERED WITH SKIN.

Windows

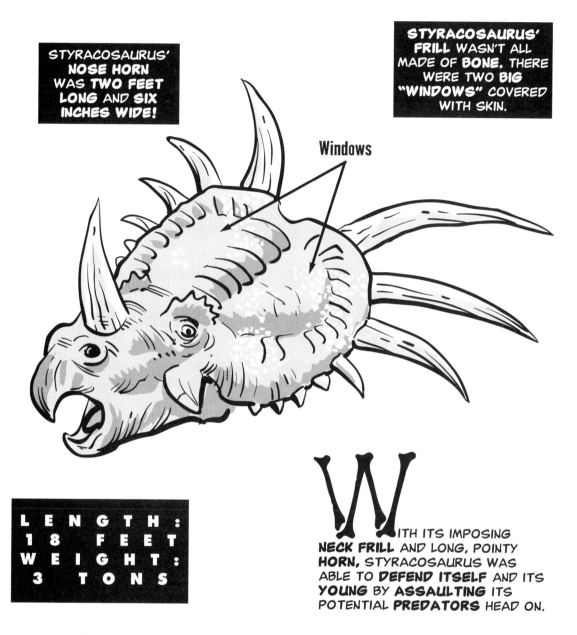

L E N G T H : 1 8 F E E T W E I G H T : 3 T O N S

WITH ITS IMPOSING **NECK FRILL** AND LONG, POINTY **HORN,** STYRACOSAURUS WAS ABLE TO **DEFEND ITSELF** AND ITS **YOUNG** BY **ASSAULTING** ITS POTENTIAL **PREDATORS** HEAD ON.

Footnote: Styracosaurus laid eggs and cared for its young.

DIG IT

Styracosaurus was first discovered by Canadian paleontologist Lawrence Lambe in 1913.

Lawrence Lambe

Lawrence Lambe (1863-1919) was a Canadian paleontologist who worked for the Geological Survey of Canada. He collaborated closely with the Sternberg team, a family of dinosaur hunters composed of Charles Sternberg and his three sons, George, Charlie, and Levi.

The Sternberg team supplied Lambe with fossils, and on one occasion with a mummy of Edmontosaurus. Thanks to the Sternbergs' discoveries and Lambe's scientific genius, much was learned about Edmontosaurus.

Lambeosaurus was named after Lambe.

Edmontosourus, the "Lizard from Edmonton," was studied in depth by Lambe.

Lambe didn't rely solely on the fossils shipped to him by the Sternberg team. He often went on his own expeditions. His discoveries include many dinosaurs like Chasmosaurus, Edmontosaurus, and Styracosaurus.

In 1923, to honor Lambe's work and dedication, paleontologist William Parks named a newly discovered dinosaur Lambeosaurus.

AMARGASAURUS

ah-mahr-ga-sore-us   *"Lizard from La Amarga"*

AMARGASAURUS WAS A **HERBIVORE** AND HAD A **DOUBLE ROW** OF **SPINES** RUNNING DOWN ITS **NECK.** THE **SPINES** COULD BE AS LONG AS **ONE-AND-A-HALF FEET!**

TRIASSIC • JURASSIC • CRETACEOUS

WAS THERE **SKIN** BETWEEN **AMARGASAURUS'** SPINES? SCIENTISTS ARE STILL **DEBATING!**

Skin

LENGTH: 33 FEET WEIGHT: 5.5 TONS

PALEONTOLOGIST **LEONARDO SALGADO** REPORTED THAT **AMARGASAURUS** WAS THE **FIRST DINOSAUR** FROM THE **EARLY CRETACEOUS PERIOD** TO BE DISCOVERED. IT SHOWED **LINKS** WITH OTHER **DINOSAURS** FROM **AFRICA** (AT THAT TIME, **AFRICA** AND **SOUTH AMERICA** WERE **JOINED**). THIS FINDING INITIATED A **RUSH** OF **NEW INTERPRETATIONS** AND **STUDIES** ON **SOUTH AMERICAN DINOSAURS.**

AMARGASAURUS SHARED WITH ITS **AFRICAN RELATIVES** A **HOLE** IN THE **ROOF** OF ITS **SKULL** OF **UNCERTAIN FUNCTION.**

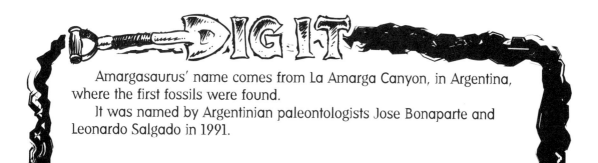

DIG IT

Amargasaurus' name comes from La Amarga Canyon, in Argentina, where the first fossils were found.

It was named by Argentinian paleontologists Jose Bonaparte and Leonardo Salgado in 1991.

INTERVIEW WITH ARGENTINIAN PALEONTOLOGIST
LEONARDO SALGADO

LEONARDO SALGADO IS A **PALEONTOLOGIST** FOR THE **MUSEUM OF GEOLOGY AND PALEONTOLOGY** OF THE **NATIONAL UNIVERSITY OF COMAHUE** IN BUENOS AIRES, ARGENTINA. WE ASKED HIM SOME **QUESTIONS** ABOUT HIS **WORK** AND **DINOSAURS.**

WHY DO **PALEONTOLOGISTS** CHOSE A CERTAIN **LOCATION** FOR A **DINOSAUR HUNT EXPEDITION?**

WE KNOW CERTAIN **INFORMATION.** FOR INSTANCE, WE KNOW THE **AGE** OF THE **ROCKS** FROM **GEOLOGICAL STUDIES.** AND WE KNOW OF THE EXISTENCE OF **FOSSILS** FROM THE **LOCAL PEOPLE.**

WHO GOES ON THE **EXPEDITION?**

PALEONTOLOGISTS, GEOLOGISTS, TECHNICIANS, AND **VOLUNTEERS.** THE **PALEONTOLOGIST** IS NORMALLY IN CHARGE OF THE **EXPEDITION.**

NO, I DON'T (PERHAPS
I **SHOULD...!**)

Salgado's discovery of
Giganotosaurus broke
T. rex's long-standing record
as the biggest meat-eater
ever to walk on land.

HOW DO **DINOSAUR FOSSILS** GET **DISCOVERED?**

WELL, WE JUST **WALK** AROUND **WATCHING** CAREFULLY.
WE DON'T HAVE ANY **SPECIAL METHODS.**

ONCE YOU FIND SOMETHING YOU THINK IS A **DINOSAUR FOSSIL,** WHAT DO YOU DO?

WE EVALUATE THE **DEGREE** OF **PRESERVATION,** TAKE **PICTURES,** AND **MARK** THE **SITE.** WE ALSO TAKE SOME **NOTES.**

ONCE THESE FOSSILS ARE IN THE **MUSEUM LAB** HOW DO YOU **FIGURE OUT** WHAT **DINOSAUR** THEY **BELONG** TO?

WELL, IF YOU FIND A **DOG'S SKULL** IN THE STREET, YOU CAN GET AN **IDEA** OF THE **WHOLE ANIMAL** BECAUSE YOU KNOW OTHER "**COMPLETE" DOGS.** IN OUR CASE, WE HAVE ACCESS TO MANY **WELL-PRESERVED SKELETONS** OF DIFFERENT KINDS OF **DINOSAURS** IN ARGENTINA AND IN OTHER COUNTRIES. SO, IF WE FIND ONLY A **BONE** OF A **DINOSAUR,** WE CAN REFER (NOT ALWAYS WITHOUT **DOUBTS)** TO A **WELL-KNOWN GROUP** OF **DINOSAURS.**

Leonardo Salgado thought the spines on Amargasaurus' neck and back functioned as defensive weapons.

HOW DO YOU **FIGURE OUT** THAT THE **FOSSILS** YOU HAVE FOUND BELONG TO AN **UNKNOWN DINOSAUR?**

WE COMPARE THE **FOSSILS** WITH **OTHERS.** WE VISIT **MUSEUMS** AND READ A LOT OF **PALEONTOLOGICAL PAPERS** UNTIL WE ARE **SURE** THAT OUR **DINOSAUR** IS A **NEW ONE.** IT OFTEN HAPPENS THAT A **"NEW"** DINOSAUR WAS NAMED FROM A **SKELETON** WITH ONLY A FEW BONES, AND LATER SOME OTHER PALEONTOLOGIST REALIZED THAT THOSE **BONES** BELONGED TO A **SPECIES ALREADY KNOWN.**

PALEONTOLOGIST **JOSE BONAPARTE** AND YOU HAVE NAMED A BRAND NEW DINOSAUR, **AMARGASAURUS.** WHAT MADE YOU **NAME** IT THAT WAY?

THERE ARE NO **SPECIFIC RULES** FOR CHOOSING A **NEW NAME.** JUST RULES FOR THE **"CONSTRUCTION"** OF THE NAME (THE WORDS MUST BE IN **LATIN,** FOR INSTANCE).

MOST OF THE TIME, **DINOSAUR NAMES** REFER TO THE **SITE** WHERE THE **FOSSIL** WAS **FOUND,** OR TO THE **PEOPLE** WHO FOUND THE **BONES,** OR TO A **SPECIAL CHARACTERISTIC** OF THE **ANIMAL.**

AMARGASAURUS MEANS **"LIZARD FROM LA AMARGA,"** THE **SITE** WHERE IT WAS **FOUND.** THE SPECIFIC NAME **AMARGASAURUS CAZAUI** IS FOR **CAZAU,** THE **NAME** OF A **GEOLOGIST** WHO WORKED FOR **MANY YEARS** IN THE AREA.

GIGANOTOSAURUS

gig-ah-not-oh-sawr-us **"Giant Southern Lizard"**

GIGANOTOSAURUS HAD A **KEEN SENSE** OF **SMELL, SHARP SERRATED TEETH, CLAWED HANDS,** AND A **HUGE MOUTH.** IT WAS SO **STRONG** IT COULD KILL **PREY** MUCH **BIGGER** THAN ITSELF.

GIGANOTOSAURUS BROKE T. REX'S LONG-STANDING RECORD OF BEING THE **BIGGEST MEAT-EATING DINOSAUR!**

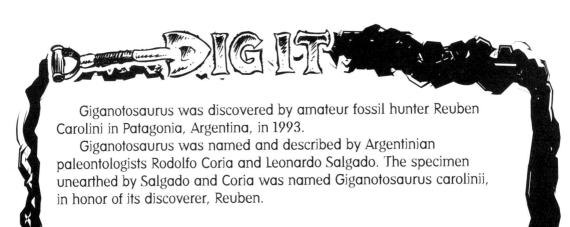

DIG IT

Giganotosaurus was discovered by amateur fossil hunter Reuben Carolini in Patagonia, Argentina, in 1993.

Giganotosaurus was named and described by Argentinian paleontologists Rodolfo Coria and Leonardo Salgado. The specimen unearthed by Salgado and Coria was named Giganotosaurus carolinii, in honor of its discoverer, Reuben.

GIGANOTOSAURUS AND **CARCHARODONTOSAURUS**, AN AFRICAN CARNIVORE, WERE SO **SIMILAR** SCIENTISTS THINK THEY MAY HAVE BEEN THE **SAME DINOSAUR.** THIS THEORY COULD BE RIGHT AS **SOUTH AMERICA** AND **AFRICA** WERE **ATTACHED** DURING THE **CRETACEOUS PERIOD,** WHEN **BOTH** THESE **DINOSAURS** LIVED.

Footnote: Giganotosaurus lived about 90 million years ago. It was extinct by the time T. rex evolved.

LENGTH:
45 FEET
HEIGHT:
12 FEET
WEIGHT:
8 TONS

SCALE

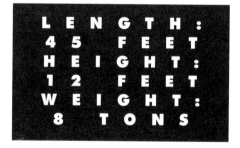

TRIASSIC   JURASSIC   CRETACEOUS

TYRANNOSAURUS REX

tee-run-oh-sawr-us rex   *"Tyrant Lizard King"*

UNTIL RECENTLY, TYRANNOSAURUS REX, OR **T. REX,** WAS THE **BIGGEST MEAT-EATING DINOSAUR** EVER KNOWN! IT WAS AS HEAVY AS A **TANK** AND AS LONG AS A **CITY BUS!** THAT'S WHY IT WAS GIVEN THE ROYAL NAME OF **"TYRANT LIZARD KING!"**

ALTHOUGH VERY POWERFULLY BUILT, **T. REX** HAD **TINY ARMS—** THEY WERE AS LONG AS **YOURS,** BUT **T. REX** WAS **TEN FEET HIGH!** ONLY **THREE FEET LONG,** ITS **ARMS** DIDN'T EVEN REACH ITS **MOUTH!** THEY WERE PROBABLY USED TO KEEP **CAPTURED PREY** STILL, BUT NOT TO GRASP SINCE THEY HAD ONLY **TWO FINGERS!**

Footnote: In 1993, T. rex's record was broken: an even bigger and more massive carnivorous dinosaur was discovered. It was named Giganotosaurus!

SNEAKY SCAVENGER.
SOME SCIENTISTS THINK T. REX'S **ARMS** WERE **TOO SMALL** TO BREAK A **FALL.** IF IT FELL, **T. REX** WOULD HAVE **CRASHED** TO THE GROUND, CAUSING **SERIOUS INJURY.** BECAUSE OF THIS, T. REX MOVED **VERY SLOWLY** AND COULDN'T **CHASE** ITS **PREY,** SO INSTEAD IT FED ON **CARCASSES.**

POWERFUL PREDATOR.
ON THE OTHER HAND, SOME SCIENTISTS OBSERVED **HEALED BONE FRACTURES** AND ARGUE **T. REX** WAS ABLE TO TAKE A **TUMBLE** OR TWO. THEY BELIEVE T. REX COULD **RUN FAST** FOR A **SHORT** PERIOD OF **TIME,** AND FED ON **YOUNG** OR **SICK ANIMALS,** WHICH WERE LESS LIKELY TO **ESCAPE.**

TYRANNOSAURUS REX

T. REX HAD A VERY KEEN **SENSE** OF **SMELL,** WHICH HELPED IT FIND OUT WHERE ITS **PREY** WAS **HIDING.**

A STIFF TAIL BALANCED T. REX'S **MASSIVE HEAD.**

WEIGHT: 5 TONS

HEIGHT: 10 FEET

LENGTH: 40 FEET

SCALE

ITS **BITE** WAS SO **POWERFUL,** IT WAS ABLE TO **CRUSH** THE **BONES** OF ITS **PREY.**

TRIASSIC ● **JURASSIC** ● **CRETACEOUS**

X-RAY VISUALIZATION

Look at this page while holding it up to a window to see T. rex's skeleton!

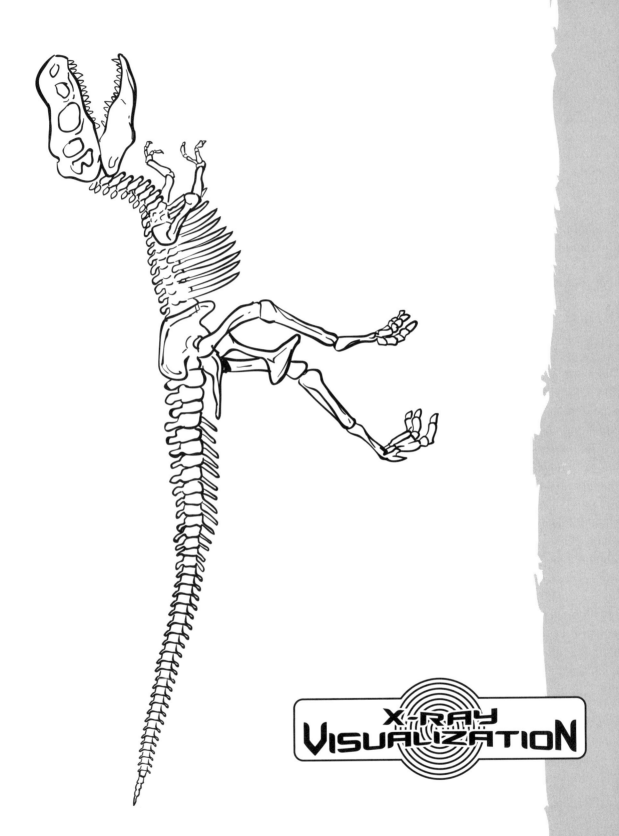

X-RAY
VISUALIZATION

IN 1990, THE MOST **COMPLETE** SKELETON OF **T. REX** WAS FOUND IN A **FARM FIELD** IN SOUTH DAKOTA. THE FARMER ACUTIONED IT, AND THE **FIELD MUSEUM** BOUGHT IT FOR A WHOPPING **$8.36 MILLION!**

T. **REX'S JAW** WAS **FOUR FEET** LONG AND COULD **DISLOCATE**, LIKE A SNAKE'S. T. REX WOULD **BITE** ITS VICTIM WITH ITS **KNIFE-LIKE TEETH**, SHAKE ITS **HEAD** TO RIP A **HUGE CHUNK** OF MEAT OFF, AND **SWALLOW** IT WITHOUT **CHEWING.**

ITS **TEETH** WERE **FIVE INCHES** LONG WITH **SAW-LIKE EDGES** AND **GREW BACK** WHEN THEY WORE OUT.

DIG IT

The first T. rex was found by legendary fossil hunter Barnum Brown in 1902, while on an expedition for the American Museum of Natural History.

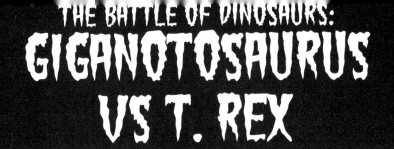

THE BATTLE OF DINOSAURS:
GIGANOTOSAURUS
VS T. REX

Giganotosaurus
Place: South America
(maybe Africa)
Skull Length: 6 feet
Hands: with 3 fingers
Height: 12 feet
Length: 45 feet
Weight: 8 tons
Brain: very small

T. rex
Place: North America
Skull Length: 5 feet
Hands: with 2 fingers
Height: 10 feet
Length: 40 feet
Weight: 5 tons
Brain: small,
but bigger than
Giganotosaurus

THESE TWO **DINOSAURS** NEVER MET **FACE-TO-FACE. GIGANOTOSAURUS** WAS **EXTINCT** BY THE TIME **T. REX EVOLVED.**
BUT IF THESE TWO **MEAT-GULPING MONSTERS** WERE TO **FIGHT** EACH OTHER, WHO WOULD **WIN? YOU DECIDE!**

DEINONYCHUS

die-non-i-kus   *"Terrible Claw"*

DEINONYCHUS MEANS **"TERRIBLE CLAW."** IT GOT ITS NAME BECAUSE OF THE **SIX INCH SPUR** ON ITS **TOE.** THE CLAW **POINTED UP** WHILE THIS DINOSAUR WAS **RUNNING,** AND IT WAS USED TO **SLASH** AT ITS **PREY** DURING **ATTACKS.**

SCALE

LENGTH: 10 FEET
HEIGHT: 6 FEET
WEIGHT: 140 LBS

DIG IT

In 1969, for the first time in paleontology, John Ostrom described Deinonychus as a very active and agile hunter. This ground-breaking theory countered the common assumption that dinosaurs were sluggish and lumbering animals. He also suggested that dinosaurs might have been warm-blooded.

DEINONYCHUS HUNTED **IN PACKS** TO **BRING DOWN** PREY **MUCH BIGGER** THEN AN **INDIVIDUAL HUNTER.** SURROUNDING THEIR **VICTIM,** EACH DEINONYCHUS **SLASHED** AT IT WITH ONE **FOOT SPUR,** WHILE **BALANCING** ON THE OTHER FOOT. WITH THEIR **CLAWS,** DEINONYCHUS HELD THEIR **VICTIM,** MAKING IT IMPOSSIBLE FOR IT TO **ESCAPE. TIRED** BY THEIR **STRUGGLE** AND LOSS OF **BLOOD,** THE **PREY** WOULD **FALL** AND BE **EATEN.**

Footnote: Deinonychus' tail was very stiff and was used for balance during runs and leaps.

CORYTHOSAURUS

kohr-ith-oh-sawr-us **"Helmet Lizard"**

CORYTHOSAURUS' MOST
IMPRESSIVE **CHARACTERISTIC**
WAS ITS **CREST** THAT
RESEMBLED A **HELMET.**

● **TRIASSIC** ● **JURASSIC** ● **CRETACEOUS**

CORYTHOSAURUS' **NOSTRILS** WENT ALL THE WAY UP INTO ITS **CREST**, SO IT IS POSSIBLE THAT CORYTHOSAURUS HAD A VERY DEVELOPED **SENSE OF SMELL**.

IT'S PROBABLE THAT CORYTHOSAURUS USED ITS **CREST** TO MAKE **SOUNDS**.

CORYTHOSAURUS LIVED IN **HERDS**. BY BLOWING **LOUD SOUNDS** THROUGH ITS CREST, CORYTHOSAURUS WAS ABLE TO **WARN** TO THE OTHER MEMBERS OF THE **GROUP** OF **IMPENDING DANGER** IF THE **HERD** WAS UNDER **ATTACK**. DIFFERENT **SOUNDS** COULD HAVE BEEN USED TO DECLARE A MEMBER'S **RANK** WITHIN THE GROUP, OR FOR **COURTSHIP**.

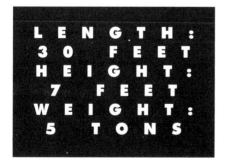

LENGTH: 30 FEET
HEIGHT: 7 FEET
WEIGHT: 5 TONS

SCALE

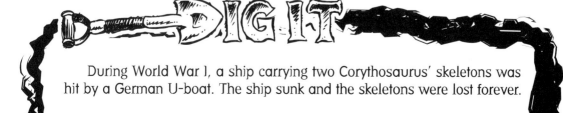

DIG IT

During World War 1, a ship carrying two Corythosaurus' skeletons was hit by a German U-boat. The ship sunk and the skeletons were lost forever.

Edward Drinker Cope

Edward Drinker Cope (1840–1897) was a zoologist at Haverford College, a professor at the University of Pennsylvania, and a curator of the National Museum in Washington, D.C. He named over 2,000 species of animals and wrote over 1,600 scientific papers.

He theorized that, with the passage of time, animal species become bigger. His theory was called "Cope's Law," but turned out to be unsubstantiated.

The American Society of Ichthyologists and Herpetologists still publishes a journal named "Copeia," to honor Cope's work on reptiles.

Camarasaurus is one of the many animals Cope described and named.

At his death, Cope donated his body for scientific research. His body became the "type specimen" for Homo sapiens, or humans. In other words, he is the original individual against which others are compared to establish if they belong to the human species.

Othniel Charles Marsh

Othniel Charles Marsh (1831-1899) was the son of a farmer, but had a very rich uncle, George Peabody. With his uncle's money, Marsh founded the Yale Peabody Museum and became a professor at Yale University.

Marsh discovered and named many extinct animals, including 25 dinosaur genera. In his haste to name more dinosaurs than competing paleontologist Edward Drinker Cope (see previous page), Marsh committed several errors. In one case, he mistakenly put a Camarasaurus' skull on a skeleton of Apatosaurus, where it remained until 1970.

Marsh went on several expeditions to the western United States looking for fossils. On one occasion, he gained permission from the Native American Chief Red Cloud of the Lakota to dig for fossils on the tribe's sacred grounds. In exchange for this generosity, Marsh went to President Grant and advocated for and won better treatment for the Lakota tribe.

Allosaurus was one of the many dinosaurus named by Marsh.

COMO BLUFF, WYOMING. COPE AND MARSH ARE BOTH DIGGING FOR FOSSILS. THE RIVAL CAMPS ARE ONLY A FEW MILES FROM EACH OTHER.
THEN ONE NIGHT...
HERE THEY ARE—!
TO THE HORSES!
... MARSH STEALS COPE'S FOSSILS!
STOP, THIEVES!
5.

TIME AFTER TIME...

Today

Cretaceous

Triceratops

Nodosaurus

Hypsilophodon

Allosaurus

Cetiosaurus

Anchisaurus

Dilophosaurus

Jurassic

Plateosaurus

Triassic

NOT ALL **DINOSAURS** LIVED AT THE **SAME TIME!** THE **MESOZOIC ERA** LASTED FOR **185 MILLION YEARS.** DURING SUCH A LONG TIME, MANY SPECIES **EVOLVED** AND BECAME **EXTINCT.** DO YOU KNOW THERE'S **MORE TIME** BETWEEN **STEGOSAURUS** AND **T. REX** THAN BETWEEN **T. REX** AND **YOU?**

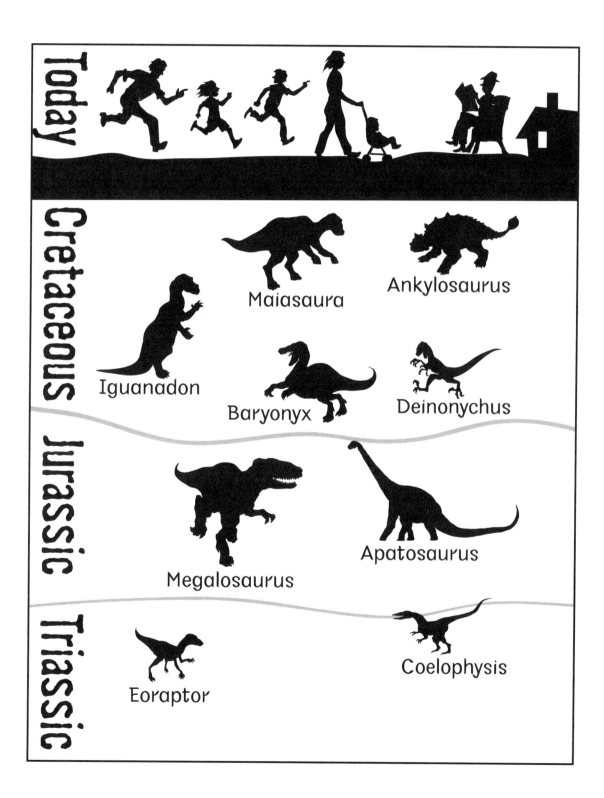

OURANOSAURUS

oo-rahn-oh-sawr-us   *"Fearless (Monitor) Lizard"*

THIS DINOSAUR'S **NAME** COMES FROM THE **TUAREG,** A **TRIBE** THAT LIVES IN **NIGER,** AFRICA, WHERE THE FIRST **OURANOSAURUS** WAS FOUND. IN THE TUAREG'S LANGUAGE **"OURANE"** IS THE **"MONITOR LIZARD,"** A LARGE REPTILE THAT LIVES IN THE DESERT. THE TUAREG **"OURANE"** IS DERIVED FROM THE ARABIC **"WARAN,"** WHICH MEANS **"FEARLESS."** SO **OURANOSAURUS** IS A **"FEARLESS MONITOR"** (OURANE) **"LIZARD"** (SAURUS).

SCALE

●   TRIASSIC   ●   JURASSIC   ●   CRETACEOUS

X-RAY VISUALIZATION

Look at this page while holding it up to a window to see Ouranosaurus' skeleton!

X-RAY VISUALIZATION

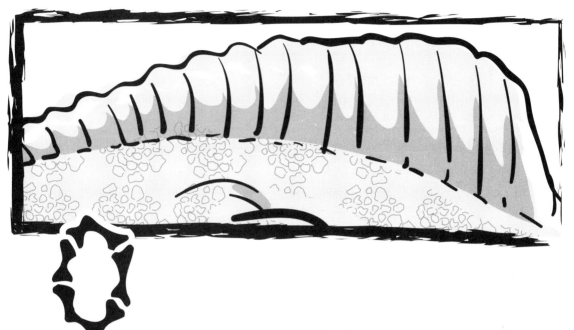

URANOSAURUS HAD A **LONG SAIL** RUNNING DOWN ITS **BACK.** SOME PALEONTOLOGISTS THINK THAT THE SAIL REGULATED OURANOSAURUS' **BODY TEMPERATURE.** BY TURNING ITS SAIL TO OR FROM THE **SUN,** OURANOSAURUS COULD **WARM** ITSELF **UP** OR COOL **DOWN.**

SOME OTHER SCIENTISTS THINK THAT IF **THREATENED,** OURANOSAURUS **STRAIGHTENED** AND **CHANGED** ITS SAIL'S **COLOR.** THIS **DISPLAY** WOULD SCARE ITS **PREDATORS** AWAY.

ONE FINAL THEORY IS THAT THE **SIZE** AND **COLOR** OF THE SAIL WAS A **SILENT MESSAGE** CONVEYING OURANOSAURUS' **GENDER, AGE,** AND **RANK.** KIND OF LIKE CARRYING A HUGE **PHOTO ID** ON YOUR BACK!

LENGTH: 23 FEET

DIG IT

The most complete skeleton of Ouranosaurus was found by a French-Italian expedition. It was organized by Giancarlo Ligabue from the Venice Museum of Natural History, and Philippe Taquet from the Paris Museum of Natural History.

In 1973 they found a huge cemetery of many dinosaur and reptile species in the Tenere Desert in Niger. Taquet named Ouranosaurus in 1976.

HYPSILOPHODON

hip-si-lo-foh-don "*High-Ridge Tooth*"

YPSILOPHODON WAS **HERBIVOROUS.** IT HAD A **BEAK** TO TORE OFF **LEAVES** AND **PLANTS.** IT ALSO HAD **SELF-SHARPENING TEETH** TO **CHEW** THE VEGETATION WITH.

● **TRIASSIC** ● **JURASSIC** ● **CRETACEOUS**

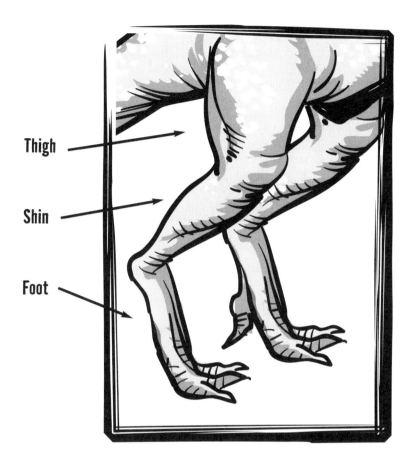

Thigh

Shin

Foot

VERY LONG FEET AND **SHINS** (LONGER THAN ITS **THIGHS**) MADE **HYPSILOPHODON** A **SPRINTER** AND **FAST RUNNER**. IN **SLOW-MOVING ANIMALS**, THE **RELATIONSHIP** BETWEEN **SHINS** AND **THIGHS** IS **INVERTED**: THE **THIGHS** ARE **LONGER** THAN THE **SHINS**.

HYPSILOPHODON COULD RUN UP TO **20 MILES** PER **HOUR!**

HYPSILOPHODON LIVED IN **HERDS** AND WAS ALWAYS ON THE **LOOKOUT** FOR **POSSIBLE PREDATORS**. WHEN FACED WITH **DANGER**, HYPSILOPHODON'S **ONLY DEFENSE** WAS TO **RUN AS FAST AS IT COULD.**

LENGTH: 6 FEET
WEIGHT: 50 LBS

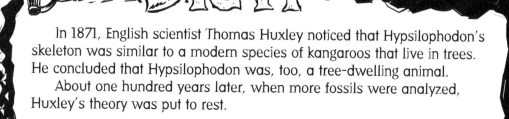

DIG IT

In 1871, English scientist Thomas Huxley noticed that Hypsilophodon's skeleton was similar to a modern species of kangaroos that live in trees. He concluded that Hypsilophodon was, too, a tree-dwelling animal.

About one hundred years later, when more fossils were analyzed, Huxley's theory was put to rest.

Many animals that are now extinct lived at the same time as dinosaurs. Here are some of the weirder-looking ones!

PTERODACTYLUS

ar-kee-op-ter-iks

"Wing Finger"

PTERODACTYLUS WAS A **FLYING REPTILE** TWO AND A HALF FEET LONG. IT LIVED DURING THE **JURASSIC PERIOD** IN **TANZANIA** AND **EUROPE**. PTERODACTYLUS WASN'T COVERED WITH **FEATHERS**, BUT, LIKE MODERN BIRDS, HAD **HOLLOW BONES**, WHICH MADE IT **LIGHT** AND CAPABLE OF **FLYING**.

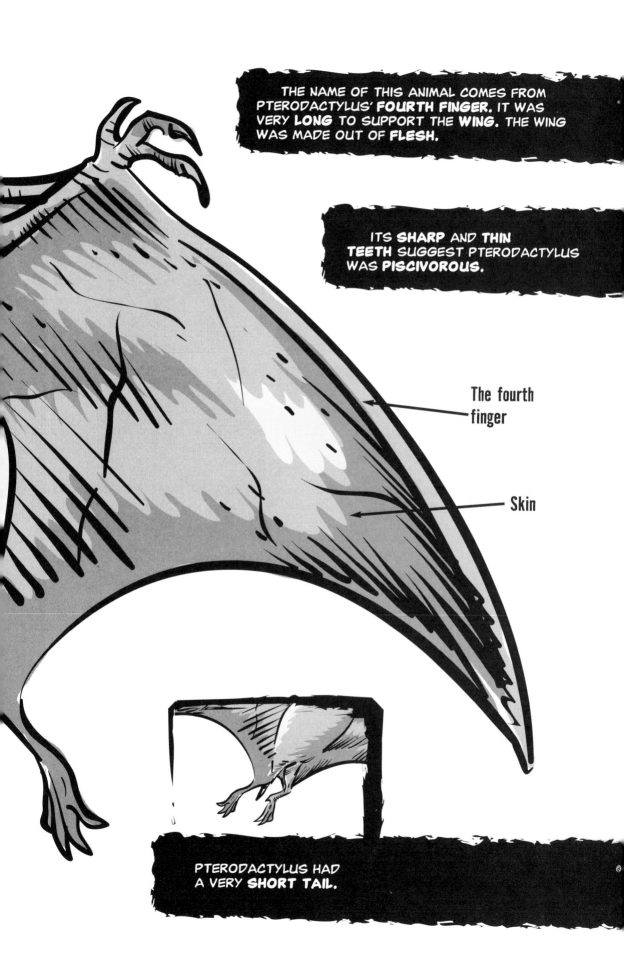

THE NAME OF THIS ANIMAL COMES FROM PTERODACTYLUS' **FOURTH FINGER.** IT WAS VERY **LONG** TO SUPPORT THE **WING.** THE WING WAS MADE OUT OF **FLESH.**

ITS **SHARP** AND **THIN** **TEETH** SUGGEST PTERODACTYLUS WAS **PISCIVOROUS.**

The fourth finger

Skin

PTERODACTYLUS HAD A VERY **SHORT TAIL.**

EGGS!

Some dinosaurs half-buried their eggs in the ground. In this way, the eggs were protected from climate changes and hidden from predators.

Some dinosaurs sat on their nests like modern hens.

Other dinosaurs covered their nests with plants. When the plants began rotting, they released heat and kept the eggs warm.

IN 1859 IN FRANCE, GEOLOGIST **JEAN JACQUES POUECH** DISCOVERED THE **FIRST** FOSSILIZED DINOSAUR **EGGS.** THEY WERE THOUGHT TO BELONG TO A **HUGE BIRD** UNTIL 1877, WHEN FRENCH PALEONTOLOGIST **PAUL GERVAIS** DECLARED THEY BELONGED TO **HYPSELOSAURUS,** A **SAUROPOD** LIKE **APATOSAURUS.**

IN 1924, **ROY CHAPMAN ANDREWS' EXPEDITION** TO THE **GOBI DESERT** FOUND THE **FIRST NESTS.** HE MISTAKENLY ASSIGNED THEM TO **PROTOCERATOPS.** THE NESTS WERE **OVIRAPTOR'S** INSTEAD. SINCE THEN, SEVERAL **FOSSILIZED EGGS** AND **NESTS** HAVE BEEN DISCOVERED, BUT FEW CONTAINED BABY **DINOSAURS.**

PERHAPS THE MOST FAMOUS **DISCOVERY** WAS MADE IN THE **SEVENTIES**, WHEN SEVERAL **MAIASAURA'S NESTS, EGGS, BABIES** AND **ADULTS** WERE FOUND.

THE DISCOVERY INDICATED THAT YEAR AFTER YEAR, **HERDS** OF MAIASAURA RETURNED TO THE **SAME PLACE** TO **LAY** THEIR **EGGS**. THEIR **NESTS** WERE BUILT **CLOSE ENOUGH** TO EACH OTHER TO BE **DEFENDED**, BUT **FAR ENOUGH** FOR THE **ADULTS** TO **MOVE AROUND** THEM.

SCIENTISTS NOTICED THE **HATCHLINGS' TEETH** WERE WORN WITH **USE**. THEY THINK THE **BABY DINOSAURS** HAD BEEN **EATING** WHILE THEY WERE STILL IN THEIR **NESTS**. THE ADULTS MUST HAVE BEEN **FEEDING** AND **CARING** FOR THEM, LIKE MODERN BIRDS, UNTIL THEY WERE **STRONG** ENOUGH TO **FEND** FOR THEMSELVES.

 Footnote: Not all dinosaurs were as caring as Maiasaura, because some dinosaur hatchlings didn't need help at all. Once out of the eggs, the baby dinosaurs would leave their nest looking for food on their own.

POLACANTHUS

pol-ah-kan-thus   *"Many Spikes"*

P OLACANTHUS' NAME MEANS "**MANY SPIKES**" AND REFERS TO THE SEVERAL **SPINES** POLACANTHUS HAD ON ITS **HEAD, SHOULDERS,** AND **HALF** OF ITS **BACK.** THE OTHER HALF OF ITS **BACK** WAS COVERED BY A **BONY ARMOR.** POLACANTHUS HAD SEVERAL **FLAT SPINES** ON ITS **TAIL,** TOO.

SCALE

POLACANTHUS' BACK WAS ITS MAIN DEFENSE AGAINST PREDATORS. AS WITH ALL THE OTHER ARMORED DINOSAURS, IF POLACANTHUS WAS ATTACKED, IT WOULD IMMEDIATELY SQUAT ON THE GROUND. IN THIS POSITION, ITS BELLY, THE MOST VULNERABLE PART OF ITS BODY, WOULD BE PROTECTED. AT THE SAME TIME, POLACANTHUS' EXPOSED BACK, WITH ITS BONY ARMOR AND MANY SPIKES, WOULD BE IMPOSSIBLE FOR A PREDATOR TO BITE.

VERY FEW POLACANTHUS FOSSILS WERE EVER FOUND, SO WE DON'T KNOW FOR SURE HOW THE SPIKES WERE ARRANGED ON ITS BACK.

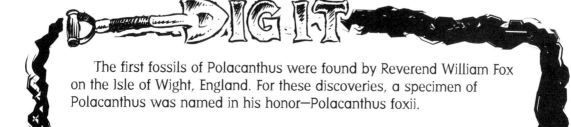

DIG IT

The first fossils of Polacanthus were found by Reverend William Fox on the Isle of Wight, England. For these discoveries, a specimen of Polacanthus was named in his honor—Polacanthus foxii.

TYRANNOSAURUS YUKs!

13. WHICH **DINOSAUR** KNOWS THE **MOST** ABOUT **SYNONYMS** AND **ANTONYMS?**

—THE-SAURUS!

14. WHAT DO YOU **GET** WHEN YOU **CROSS COELOPHYSIS** WITH **FIREWORKS?**

—DINO-MITE!

15. WHAT DO **YOU** CALL **SOMETHING** YOU SHOULD **NEVER DO** TO AN **IGUANODON?**

—AN IGUANO**DON'T!**

16. WHAT IS **BROWN,** HAS **HANDLES,** AND IS **FULL** OF **DINOSAURS** WITH **HORNS** ON THEIR **NOSES?**

—A **BAG**-A-**CERATOPS!**

17. WHICH DINOSAUR IS THE **FATEST?**

—A **PRONTO**-SAURS!

 **18.** WHICH **DINOSAUR** CASTS SPELLS?

—THE TYRANNOSAURUS **HEX!**

ANKYLOSAURUS

an-ky-loh-sawr-us   *"Fused Lizard"*

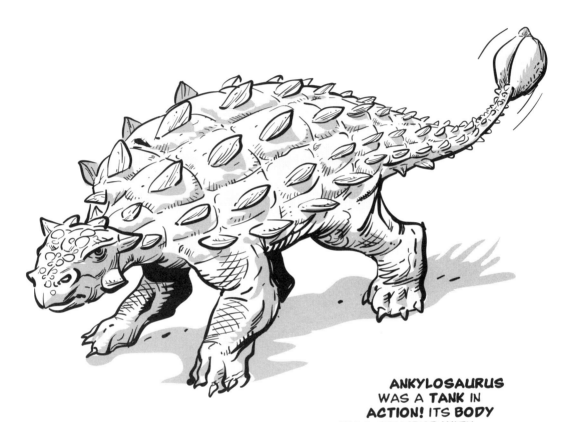

ANKYLOSAURUS WAS A **TANK** IN **ACTION!** ITS **BODY** WAS COVERED WITH **PLATES** OF **BONE** EMBEDDED IN ITS **SKIN.** THE WORD ANKYLOSAURUS MEANS **"FUSED LIZARD."** EVEN ANKYLOSAURUS' **EYELIDS** WERE PROTECTED BY **BONY PLATES.**

●   **TRIASSIC**   ●   **JURASSIC**   ●   **CRETACEOUS**

ITS **PROTECTIVE SUIT** WAS **STURDY** AND **RESISTANT** TO **ASSAULTS,** BUT **FLEXIBLE** ENOUGH SO ANKYLOSAURUS COULD MOVE FREELY.

ANKYLOSAURUS HAD BIG **SPIKES** ALONG ITS **BODY** ALL THE WAY DOWN TO ITS **TAIL,** EVEN ON ITS **CHEEKS!** A **BITE** FROM A PREDATOR WOULD HAVE BEEN MUCH MORE **DANGEROUS** FOR THE **PREDATOR!**

Footnote: Ankylosaurus could not run fast enough to escape its predators because it had short, chubby legs and a heavy body.

ANKYLOSAURUS

ANKYLOSAURUS' TAIL HAD POWERFUL **MUSCLES,** STIFF **TENDONS,** AND ENDED IN A BIG **BONY CLUB.** IF ATTACKED, **ANKYLOSAURUS** WOULD QUICKLY **SWING** ITS TAIL FROM **SIDE TO SIDE** TRYING TO **WHACK** ITS PREDATOR. ANKYLOSAURUS WAS SO POWERFUL THAT A **STUNNING BLOW** COULD **BREAK** ITS ENEMY'S BONES.

HEIGHT: 4 FEET

WEIGHT: 4 TONS

LENGTH: 30 FEET

DIG IT

Ankylosaurus was first named by famous fossil hunter Barnum Brown in 1908.

ANKYLOSAURUS DIDN'T HAVE ANY **PROTECTION** ON ITS BELLY. IF ITS ATTACKER **FLIPPED** IT **OVER**, ANKYLOSAURUS WOULD BE **COMPLETELY EXPOSED** AND **DEFENSELESS.**

ANKYLOSAURUS ATE **PLANTS** IT TORE WITH ITS **TOOTHLESS BEAK.** ITS **CHEEK TEETH** WERE VERY **SMALL** AND **WEAK,** SO ANKYLOSAURUS ATE **SOFT VEGETATION.**

Footnote: Fossilized trackways of Ankylosaurus have been found near the town of Sucre, Bolivia, South America.

EDMONTOSAURUS

ed-mon-toe-sawr-us   **"Lizard from Edmonton"**

IN 1908, FOSSIL HUNTERS **CHARLES, GEORGE,** AND **LEVI STERNBERG** UNEARTHED A **MUMMY** OF **EDMONTOSAURUS** IN **WYOMING.**

DURING THE UNUSUAL PROCESS OF **NATURAL MUMMIFICATION,** THE **BODY** OF THE DEAD ANIMAL DOESN'T GET **BURIED,** BUT **DRIES OUT.** UNLIKE **FOSSILIZATION,** IN A MUMMIFIED ANIMAL, **SKIN** AND **MUSCLES** ARE SOMETIMES **PRESERVED.**

THE **MUMMY** OF EDMONTOSAURUS WAS A **MAJOR FIND** FOR PALEONTOLOGISTS. THEY LEARNED HOW **MUSCLES** ARE ATTACHED TO THE **BONES** AND WHAT EDMONTOSAURUS' **SKIN** MUST HAVE LOOKED LIKE.

DIG IT

Despite the Sternbergs' discoveries of 1908, Edmontosaurus was described and named only in 1917 by Canadian paleontologist Lawrence Lambe.

EDMONTOSAURUS HAD SOME EXTRA **SKIN** ON ITS **NOSE** ENABLING IT TO **BLOW** AND MAKE **SOUNDS.**

EDMONTOSAURUS HAD A **BEAK** AND **HUNDREDS** OF **TEETH.** AS SOON AS SOME TEETH WOULD GET **WORN OUT,** OTHERS WOULD **REPLACE** THEM.

EDMONTOSAURUS HAD A **BONY RIDGE** RUNNING DOWN ITS **BACK** AND **TAIL.**

SCALE

LENGTH: 40 FEET
WEIGHT: 3 TONS

The Sternberg Team

Charles Sternberg
(1850–1943)

George Sternberg
(1883–1969)

The Sternberg team of fossil hunters was composed of Charles and his three sons, George, Charlie, and Levi. The team worked for a couple of decades at the beginning of the 1900s.

Together they found thousands of fossils during several expeditions to Alberta and Wyoming. Some of their discoveries include type specimens of Triceratops, Brachylophosaurus, and Chasmosaurus.

The type specimen for Triceratops was discovered by the Sternberg team.

George, who spotted his first Plesiosaurus fossils when he was only 10 years old, found the first mummified Edmontosaurus. Later, Charlie found a duck-billed dinosaur's mummy, too. These were enormous discoveries for paleontology because a mummy often preserves the dinosaur's muscles, tendons, entrails, and other soft-tissued organs that are lost during the process of fossilization.

The Sternberg Team

Corythosaurus had already been discovered by Barnum Brown in 1914, but the two specimens found by the Sternberg team had skin impressions.

During an expedition to Red Deer River in Alberta, Canada, the Sternberg team unearthed 25 almost complete skeletons of dinosaurs including an Albertosaurus, Triceratops, and two skeletons of Corythosaurus with skin impressions.

Levi Sternberg
(1894–1976)

Charlie Sternberg
(1885–1981)

The two skeletons of Corythosaurus were bought by the British Museum of Natural History, during World War I. The ship on which they were travelling was sunk by a German U-boat, and the skeletons were lost forever.

LAMBEOSAURUS

lamb-eeh-oh-sawr-us **"Lambe's Lizard"**

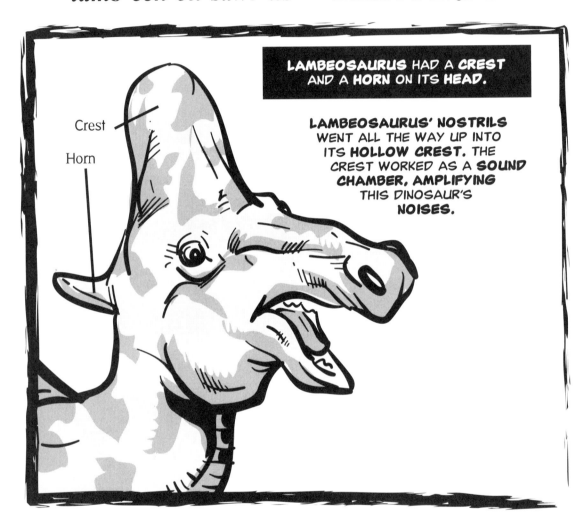

LAMBEOSAURUS HAD A **CREST** AND A **HORN** ON ITS **HEAD.**

LAMBEOSAURUS' NOSTRILS WENT ALL THE WAY UP INTO ITS **HOLLOW CREST.** THE CREST WORKED AS A **SOUND CHAMBER, AMPLIFYING** THIS DINOSAUR'S **NOISES.**

Crest

Horn

SCALE

Footnote: Lambeosaurus' horn doesn't seem to have had a function.

LENGTH: 40 FEET
WEIGHT: 5 TONS

AROUND 1905, FAMED PALEONTOLOGIST **LAWRENCE LAMBE** FOUND A FOSSILIZED DINOSAUR **SKULL**. HE MISTAKENLY THOUGHT IT BELONGED TO A DINOSAUR CALLED **STEPHANOSAURUS**.

IN 1913, DINOSAUR HUNTER **CHARLES STERNBERG** FOUND SOME **FOSSILS** AND GAVE THEM TO PALEONTOLOGIST **WILLIAM PARKS** TO ANALYZE.

WHILE **PARKS** WAS STUDYING **STERNBERG'S DISCOVERY**, HE REALIZED **LAMBE** HAD MADE A **MISTAKE**. BOTH THE **SKULL** LAMBE HAD FOUND AND THE **FOSSILS** BELONGED TO AN **UNKNOWN DINOSAUR**.

PARKS NAMED THE DINOSAUR **LAMBEOSAURUS** TO HONOR **LAMBE** AND HIS **GREAT WORK** IN PALEONTOLOGY.

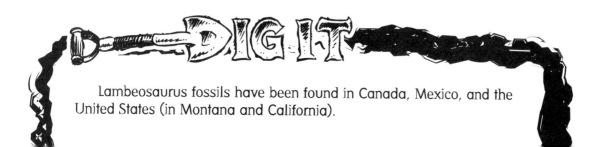

DIG IT

Lambeosaurus fossils have been found in Canada, Mexico, and the United States (in Montana and California).

BARYONYX

bah-ree-on-eeks "Heavy Claw"

I N 1983, A **PLUMBER** AND **AMATEUR FOSSIL COLLECTOR** NAMED **WILLIAM WALKER** FOUND A HUGE **CLAW** IN A **CLAY PIT** IN **SURREY,** ENGLAND. IT BELONGED TO A **DINOSAUR SKELETON** WHICH WAS LATER DUG UP. THE UNKNOWN DINOSAUR WAS NAMED **BARYONYX,** WHICH MEANS **"HEAVY CLAW."** THE **SPECIMEN** WAS NAMED **BARYONYX WALKERI** IN HONOR OF ITS FINDER **WILLIAM WALKER.**

Footnote: Baryonyx's skull was long and narrow and looked like that of a crocodile.

AFTER **WILLIAM WALKER'S DISCOVERY** OF **BARYONYX'** **CLAW,** PALEONTOLOGISTS FOR THE NATURAL MUSEUM OF LONDON ORGANIZED AN **EXPEDITION.** THEY WENT TO THE **SAME LOCATION** AND FOUND SOME BARYONYX' **BONES.**

THE PALEONTOLOGISTS NOTICED SOME **FOSSILIZED FISH** STUCK IN THE **RIBCAGE** OF THE **SKELETON,** WHERE ONCE WAS BARYONYX' **STOMACH.** THEY CONCLUDED THAT BARYONYX WAS A **PISCIVORE,** THIS PARTICULAR SPECIMEN HAD EATEN SOME **FISH** RIGHT BEFORE ITS **DEATH.**

BARYONYX HAD AT LEAST **TWICE** AS MANY **TEETH** AS ITS CONTEMPORARY **MEAT-EATING DINOSAURS.**

SCALE

LENGTH: 30 FEET
WEIGHT: 2 TONS

DIG IT

Baryonyx walkeri, the only specimen of Baryonyx ever found, was described and named by paleontologists Alan Charig and Angela Milner in 1986.

GALLIMIMUS

gal-lee-meem-us   *"Chicken-Like"*

GALLIMIMUS' SKELETON WAS VERY SIMILAR TO THAT OF A **CHICKEN** (HENCE THE NAME **"CHICKEN-LIKE"**). BUT GALLIMIMUS WAS **TWICE** AS **BIG** AS AN **OSTRICH!**

●   **TRIASSIC**   ●   **JURASSIC**   ●   **CRETACEOUS**

GALLIMIMUS DIDN'T HAVE ANY **TEETH,** ONLY A **STURDY** BEAK MUCH LIKE A **MODERN BIRD.**

GALLIMIMUS WAS ONE OF THE **FASTEST DINOSAURS,** REACHING 45 MILES PER HOUR!

SCALE

LENGTH: 20 FEET
HEIGH: 7 FEET
WEIGHT: 1 TON

DIG IT

Gallimimus was first found in Mongolia in 1972 by three paleontologists: Halszka Osmolska, Ewa Roniewicz, and Rinchen Barsbold.

IT'S ABOUT TIME!

DINOSAURS DOMINATED OUR PLANET FOR **163 MILLION YEARS** BEFORE BECOMING EXTINCT. **HUMANS** HAVE BEEN AROUND FOR **ONLY** ABOUT **100,000 YEARS.** IF THE **HISTORY** OF THE **EARTH** COULD HAPPEN IN A **24-HOUR DAY,** THIS IS HOW IT WOULD **LOOK...**

12:00 a.m. *earth is formed*

4500 million years ago

4:30 a.m. *first forms of life appears on earth*

3800 million years ago

6:00 a.m.

9:00 a.m.

12:00 p.m.

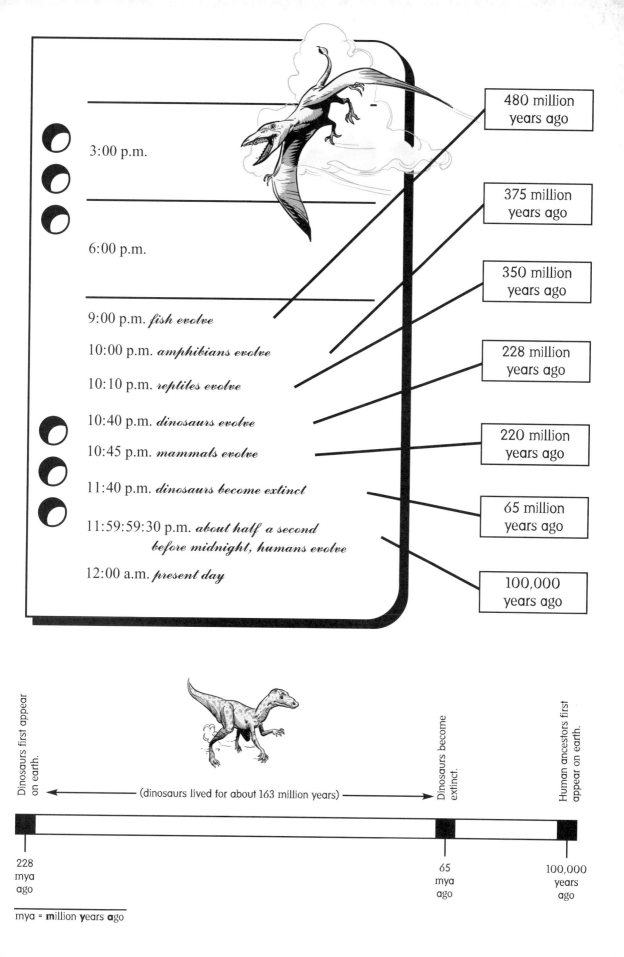

3:00 p.m.

6:00 p.m.

9:00 p.m. *fish evolve*

10:00 p.m. *amphibians evolve*

10:10 p.m. *reptiles evolve*

10:40 p.m. *dinosaurs evolve*

10:45 p.m. *mammals evolve*

11:40 p.m. *dinosaurs become extinct*

11:59:59:30 p.m. *about half a second before midnight, humans evolve*

12:00 a.m. *present day*

480 million years ago

375 million years ago

350 million years ago

228 million years ago

220 million years ago

65 million years ago

100,000 years ago

Dinosaurs first appear on earth.

Dinosaurs become extinct.

Human ancestors first appear on earth.

← (dinosaurs lived for about 163 million years) →

228 mya ago

65 mya ago

100,000 years ago

mya = **m**illion **y**ears **a**go

STATE FOSSILS

MANY **STATES** HAVE ELECTED **DINOSAURS** AND DINOSAUR'S **FOOTPRINTS** AS THEIR **OFFICIAL STATE FOSSIL!**

THE DINOSAUR **EUBRONTES** BECAME THE **CONNECTICUT STATE FOSSIL** IN 1991. NO **BONES** WERE EVER **UNEARTHED,** BUT A MAGNIFICENT **FOSSIL TRACK** OF **EUBRONTES** IS PRESERVED IN THIS STATE.

FROM THE **SHAPE** OF THE **TRACKS,** SCIENTISTS THINK **EUBRONTES** WAS RELATED TO **DILOPHOSAURUS.**

GOVERNOR **RICHARD LAMM** DECLARED **STEGOSAURUS** TO BE THE **COLORADO STATE FOSSIL** ON APRIL 28, 1982.

COELOPHYSIS BECAME THE **NEW MEXICO** STATE FOSSIL ON MARCH 17, 1981 TO COMMEMORATE **EDWIN COLBERT'S** 1947 DISCOVERY.

ON JUNE 13, 1991, **NEW JERSEY** ADOPTED **HADROSAURUS** AS THE **STATE FOSSIL.** THIS LAW COMMEMORATES **WILLIAM PARKER FOULKE'S** 1858 DISCOVERY OF THE **BEST SPECIMEN** OF **HADROSAURUS** EVER FOUND.

ON FEBRUARY 22, 1985, **MAIASAURA** BECAME THE **MONTANA STATE FOSSIL.** PALEONTOLOGISTS FOUND MANY **FOSSILIZED EGGS, BABIES** AND **ADULT MAIASAURA** IN THIS STATE. THEY THINK THIS **DINOSAUR** USED TO COME BACK **EVERY YEAR** TO THE **SAME PLACE** TO LAY ITS **EGGS.**

STATE FOSSILS

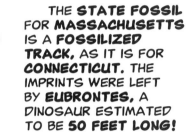

THE **STATE FOSSIL** FOR **MASSACHUSETTS** IS A **FOSSILIZED TRACK,** AS IT IS FOR **CONNECTICUT.** THE IMPRINTS WERE LEFT BY **EUBRONTES,** A DINOSAUR ESTIMATED TO BE **50 FEET LONG!**

A SERIES OF **DISCOVERIES** CULMINATING IN A MAJOR FIND OF **50 SPECIMENS** OF **ALLOSAURUS** WAS FOLLOWED BY THE **DECISION,** IN 1988, TO ADOPT THIS DINOSAUR AS **UTAH'S STATE FOSSIL.**

BRACHIOSAURUS HAS BEEN THE **TEXAS** STATE FOSSIL SINCE **1997.**

TRICERATOPS IS **SOUTH DAKOTA'S STATE FOSSIL.** THE **ACTUAL FOSSIL** IS SHOWCASED IN THE **MUSEUM OF GEOLOGY** IN **RAPID CITY.**
TRICERATOPS IS ALSO THE STATE FOSSIL OF **WYOMING,** WHERE IT WAS ADOPTED IN 1995. WYOMING'S **ACTUAL FOSSIL** IS SHOWCASED IN THE UNIVERSITY OF WYOMING GEOLOGICAL MUSEUM.

MAIASAURA

my-ah-sawr-ah   *"Good Mother Lizard"*

IN MONTANA, IN 1978, AMATEUR FOSSIL COLLECTOR **MARION BRANDVOLD** DISCOVERED SOME **FOSSILS.** THEY WERE **BABY DINOSAURS** OF AN **UNKNOWN SPECIES.** LATER, SEVERAL **NESTS, EGGS,** AND ONE **ADULT DINOSAUR** WERE FOUND IN THE SAME **SPOT.**

    JACK HORNER, CURATOR OF PALEONTOLOGY AT THE MUSEUM OF THE ROCKIES, AND ASSOCIATE **ROBERT MAKELA** SUGGESTED THIS PARTICULAR DINOSAUR TOOK CARE OF ITS **BABIES.** THIS WAS A **REVOLUTIONARY THEORY** BECAUSE **DINOSAURS,** JUST LIKE **REPTILES,** WERE BELIEVED TO **LAY EGGS** WITHOUT REARING THEIR **BABIES.**

BABY MAIASAURA WERE ABOUT **20** INCHES LONG, WHILE A **FULL-GROWN ADULT** COULD BE UP TO **40 FEET LONG!**

JACK HORNER AND **ROBERT MAKELA** NAMED THIS DINOSAUR **MAIASAURA,** A NAME COMPOSED BY THE WORDS **"MAYA"** AND **"SAURA." MAYA** WAS THE **ANCIENT GREEK GODDESS** OF THE **GOOD,** NURTURING MOTHER. **"SAURA"** IS THE FEMININE VERSION OF THE WORD **"SAURUS,"** WHICH MEANS **"LIZARD."**

IKE OTHER **DUCK-BILLED DINOSAURS,** SUCH AS **EDMONTOSAURUS** AND **CORYTHOSAURUS,** MAIASAURA WAS **QUADRUPEDAL,** BUT IF **ATTACKED,** FLED RUNNING ON ITS **TWO BACK LEGS ONLY.**

MAIASAURA

HEIGHT: 17 FEET

WEIGHT: 5 TONS

LENGTH: 40 FEET

DIG IT

Since 1978, many more fossils of Maiasaura have been found. In particular, one herd of more than 10,000 individuals of different sizes, from very small to adult, was discovered in Montana. They all died together, buried alive by a volcanic eruption.

WHEN IT WAS TIME TO **LAY EGGS,** SEVERAL **FEMALE MAIASAURA** WOULD **GROUP** TOGETHER. THEY BUILT THEIR **NESTS** VERY CLOSE TO EACH OTHER.

EACH **DINOSAUR "MOM"** WOULD MAKE A **PILE** OF **MUD,** DIG A **HOLE** ON TOP, AND DEPOSIT ABOUT **20** TO **30 EGGS.**

THE **MUD** KEPT THE **EGGS** HIDDEN FROM **PREDATORS** AND **PROTECTED** FROM THE **OUTSIDE CLIMATE.**

WHEN THE **HATCHLINGS** WERE **BORN,** THE **ADULT MAIASAURA** WOULD **FEED** AND **CARE** FOR THEM UNTIL THEY WERE **COMPLETELY DEVELOPED.**

Footnote: It is possible that Maiasaura would go back every year to the same place to deposit its eggs.

CHEW ON THIS!

SOME DINOSAURS WERE **HERBIVORES** AND FED ONLY ON **PLANTS** AND **ROOTS.** UNLIKE MEAT, **VEGETATION** HAS A **LOW NUTRITIONAL VALUE** AND TAKES **LONGER** TO DIGEST. IN ORDER TO **ASSIMILATE** AS MANY **NUTRIENTS** AS POSSIBLE FROM THE VEGETABLES THEY ATE, HERBIVOROUS DINOSAURS HAD A **VERY LONG DIGESTIVE SYSTEM.**

SAUROPODS, LIKE DIPLODOCUS, DIDN'T HAVE ANY TEETH DESIGNED FOR **CHEWING,** NOR **CHEEKS POUCHES** TO HOLD THE FOOD IN THEIR MOUTH. THEY WOULD **RIP** THE VEGETATION AND **SWALLOW** IT **WHOLE.**

THE FOOD WOULD END UP IN A **SPECIAL SACK** CALLED **GIZZARD.** THE GIZZARD CONTAINED **SMALL STONES,** UP TO **4 INCHES LONG,** THAT THE DINOSAUR HAD PREVIOUSLY SWALLOWED.

THESE STONES, CALLED **GASTROLITHS,** GROUND UP THE FOOD, BASICALLY DOING THE **CHEWING** THE TEETH COULDN'T ACCOMPLISH.

THEN THE FOOD MOVED TO THE **STOMACH,** WERE THE **DIGESTION** STARTED.

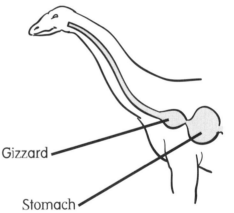

Gizzard

Stomach

Diplodocus' teeth were thin like pencils. They could strip a plant of its leaves, but could not chew.

UNLIKE SAUROPODS, **ARMORED DINOSAURS,** LIKE STEGOSAURUS, HAD **CHEEK POUCHES** AND WERE ABLE TO CHEW THEIR FOOD.

THEIR TEETH WERE IN THE SHAPE OF A **LEAF** AND NOT VERY STRONG.

IN FACT, ARMORED DINOSAURS COULD ONLY FEED ON **SOFT VEGETATION** SUCH AS **FERNS.**

DUCK-BILLED DINOSAURS, LIKE HADROSAURUS, HAD A **MULTITUDE** OF **TEETH**—AS MANY AS **2,000** IN JUST **ONE DINOSAUR'S MOUTH!** THEY HAD A **VARIED DIET** BECAUSE THEY COULD EAT EVEN THE **TOUGHEST VEGETATION** SUCH AS CONIFER NEEDLES AND ROOTS. THIS ABILITY MADE THE DUCK-BILLED DINOSAURS ONE OF THE **HARDIEST** AND MOST **WIDESPREAD DINOSAUR.**

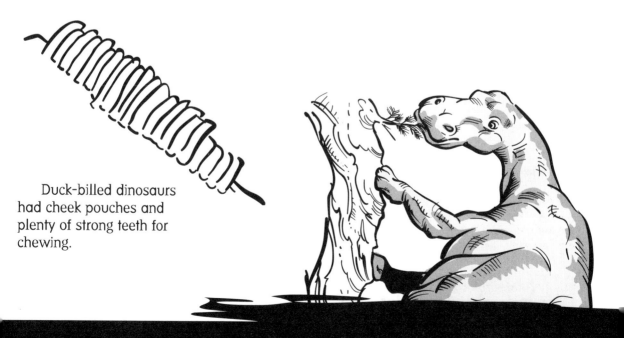

Duck-billed dinosaurs had cheek pouches and plenty of strong teeth for chewing.

DURING DIGESTION, THE **PULP** OF EATEN **PLANTS** BREAKS DOWN AND **FERMENTS.** THIS PROCESS CREATES A LOT OF **GAS.** CAN YOU IMAGINE A 15 TON DIPLODOCUS LETTING OUT A FART? STINKY!

CHEW ON THIS!

SOME DINOSAURS WERE **CARNIVORES** AND ATE OTHER **ANIMALS, EGGS, FISH** AND **INSECTS.** MEAT HAS A **HIGH NUTRITIONAL VALUE** AND TAKES **LESS TIME** TO DIGEST. CARNIVOROUS DINOSAURS HAD A **SHORTER DIGESTIVE SYSTEM** THAN HERBIVOROUS DINOSAURS.

THE **CARNIVORES' BRAIN** WAS **BIGGER** THAN THE **HERBIVORES'** EVEN WHEN THEY HAD THE **SAME BODY SIZE.** THIS MEANS THAT **CARNIVORES** WERE **SMARTER** THAN **HERBIVORES.** OTHERWISE, **CARNIVORES** WOULD NOT HAVE BEEN ABLE TO **CATCH** THEIR **PREY!**

Carnivores' teeth were sharp, often with serrated edges, like knives, to cut through their victims' flesh. They were also curved, so once the prey was bitten, it couldn't get free.

CARNIVOROUS DINOSAURS LIKE T. REX **DIDN'T CHEW** THEIR FOOD. THEY WOULD **BITE** THEIR PREY AND **RIP** A CHUNK OFF BY **SHAKING THEIR HEADS.** CARNIVORES' **TEETH** WERE **SHARP** AND THEIR **JAWS** WERE SO STRONG THEY COULD **CRUSH** THE **BONES** OF THEIR VICTIMS. AFTER BITING, CARNIVORES WOULD **SWALLOW** THE WHOLE MOUTHFUL, **WITHOUT CHEWING IT.**

SOME **DINOSAURS** PROBABLY **HUNTED** IN **PACKS.** THIS **WAY OF HUNTING** REQUIRES **MORE INTELLIGENCE** AND **COMMUNICATION SKILLS,** BUT YIELDS A **HIGH REWARD.** A **GROUP** OF **CARNIVORES** CAN **CATCH** PREY **MUCH BIGGER** THAN THEIR **INDIVIDUAL SIZE,** PROVIDING A **LARGE QUANTITY** OF **FOOD.**

RECENT DISCOVERIES INDICATE **T. REXES** FOUGHT AGAINST **EACH OTHER** FOR THE **POSSESSION** OF **FOOD**. BITE MARKS IN **FOSSILS** INDICATE SUCH **FIGHTS** MIGHT EVEN HAVE ENDED WITH THE **WINNING T. REX** EATING ITS **OPPONENT!**

T. rex's teeth were a weapon to be reckoned with!

CANNIBALISM WAS ALSO PRACTICED BY **COELOPHYSIS**, WHICH ATE ITS OWN **YOUNG** WHEN **FOOD** WAS **SCARCE**.

SOME **DINOSAURS** WERE **PISCIVOROUS**, LIKE **BARYONYX**, AND SPECIALIZED IN CATCHING **FISH** WITH THEIR **CLAWS** OR THEIR **MOUTHS**.

ORNITHOMIMIDS, BIRD-LIKE DINOSAURS LIKE **GALLIMIMUS**, DIDN'T HAVE ANY **TEETH**. INSTEAD, TO **CATCH** THEIR **PREY**, THEY USED THEIR **HARD BEAK** LIKE **MODERN BIRDS**.

SAUROPELTA

sawr-oh-pelt-ah   *"Shield Lizard"*

THIS **TANK-LIKE DINOSAUR** WAS THE BIGGEST **NODOSAURID** OF ALL MEASURING UP TO 25 FEET IN LENGHT.

ITS **BACK** WAS **COVERED** BY A **BONY SHELL** THAT WAS **EMBEDDED** IN ITS **SKIN**. THIS "ARMOR" WAS AN **EFFECTIVE PROTECTION** AGAINST **PREDATORS**.

THE BONY SHELL WAS MADE OF **SCALES** TO ALLOW **SAUROPELTA** TO **MOVE** AROUND **FREELY**.

SCALE

TRIASSIC ● **JURASSIC** ● **CRETACEOUS**

IF **ATTACKED,** SAUROPELTA WOULD **RETRACT** ITS **LEGS** UNDER ITS **BODY,** EXPOSING ITS **ARMORED BACK,** IN THE SAME WAY A **TURTLE** RETRACTS ITS **LEGS** INSIDE ITS **SHELL.**

IN THIS POSITION, **ATTACKERS** WOULD FIND IT **HARD** TO **OVERTURN** SAUROPELTA. BUT IF THEY **SUCCEEDED,** IT WOULD BE THE **END.** ITS **SOFT BELLY** WAS COMPLETELY **UNPROTECTED.** AND, JUST LIKE TURTLES, IT WAS **IMPOSSIBLE** FOR SAUROPELTA TO **FLIP** ITSELF **OVER** AGAIN!

LENGTH: 25 FEET
WEIGHT: 3 TONS

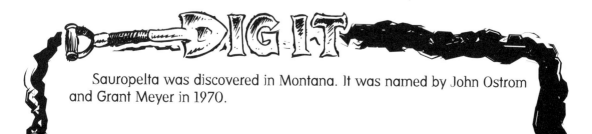

DIG IT

Sauropelta was discovered in Montana. It was named by John Ostrom and Grant Meyer in 1970.

ALBERTOSAURUS

al-bert-oh-sawr-us   *"Lizard from Alberta"*

ALBERTOSAURUS WAS A **TYRANNOSAURID**, A **GROUP** OF DINOSAURS NAMED AFTER **T. REX.**

ALBERTOSAURUS WAS ONLY ABOUT **HALF** THE **SIZE** OF **T. REX.**

SCALE

LENGTH: 26 FEET
HEIGHT: 10 FEET
WEIGHT: 20 TONS

TRIASSIC   •   JURASSIC   •   CRETACEOUS

IN 1910, DINOSAUR HUNTER **BARNUM BROWN** DISCOVERED **SEVERAL FOSSILS** IN **LITTLE SANDHILL COULEE,** IN ALBERTA, CANADA. HE DIDN'T LEAVE ANY **MAP** OF THE LOCATION—ONLY SOME **PHOTOGRAPHS.**

ABOUT **90 YEARS LATER,** CANADIAN PALEONTOLOGIST **PHILIP CURRY** FOUND BROWN'S **PHOTOGRAPHS** AND WENT IN SEARCH OF THE **LOCATION.** WHEN HE FOUND IT, HE DISCOVERED ABOUT A **DOZEN SKELETONS** OF **ALBERTOSAURUS!**

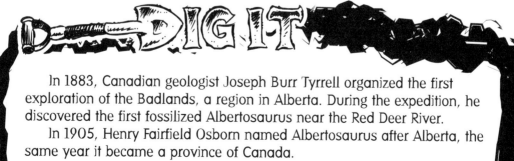

DIG IT

In 1883, Canadian geologist Joseph Burr Tyrrell organized the first exploration of the Badlands, a region in Alberta. During the expedition, he discovered the first fossilized Albertosaurus near the Red Deer River.

In 1905, Henry Fairfield Osborn named Albertosaurus after Alberta, the same year it became a province of Canada.

The Royal Tyrrell Museum (the Canadian museum of natural history) was built near the location where Albertosaurus was first discovered.

Many animals that are now extinct lived at the same time as dinosaurs. Here are some of the weirder-looking ones!

CRUSAFONTIA

crews-ah-font-eeh-uh

CRUSAFONTIA WAS A **RODENT** AND LOOKED AND BEHAVED LIKE A **MODERN SQUIRREL.** CRUSAFONTIA WAS ALSO A **MAMMAL.** DINOSAURS WERE SO **WIDESPREAD** AND **VARIED** THAT ONLY **FEW MAMMALS** LIKE CRUSAFONTIA COULD **PROLIFERATE.**

NOT VERY MUCH IS KNOWN OF THIS **TINY ANIMAL** BECAUSE **NO COMPLETE SKELETON** OF CRUSAFONTIA HAS EVER BEEN FOUND.

CRUSAFONTIA'S **TAIL** MIGHT HAVE BEEN **PREHENSILE.** THIS MEANS THAT ITS **TAIL** COULD HAVE BEEN USED FOR **GRASPING** AND **HOLDING** OBJECTS, MUCH LIKE A **MONKEY'S TAIL.**

BECAUSE OF THIS **ABILITY,** THIS LITTLE ANIMAL MIGHT HAVE BEEN ABLE TO **HANG** FROM **TREE BRANCHES** AT WILL.

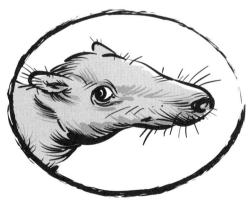

CRUSAFONTIA LIVED DURING THE **LATE TRIASSIC PERIOD,** AT THE SAME TIME AS THE DINOSAURS **COMPSOGNATHUS** AND **MEGALOSAURUS.**

FOSSILS OF CRUSAFONTIA HAVE BEEN FOUND IN **WESTERN EUROPE.**

TSINTAOSAURUS

ching-dow-sawr-us   *"Lizard from Tsintao"*

    VERY LITTLE IS KNOWN OF **TSINTAOSAURUS** AND PALEONTOLOGISTS DEBATE OVER THE PURPOSE OF ITS **ODD-LOOKING HORN.** WAS IT A **SOUND-MAKING DEVICE,** LIKE CORYTHOSAURUS' **CREST?** SHOULD IT BE **POINTING BACK** LIKE PARASAUROLOPHUS' **HORN?** SOME SCIENTISTS EVEN THINK **TSINTAOSAURUS** NEVER REALLY **EXISTED!** THEY CLAIM THE HORN WAS FOUND BY CHANCE NEAR A **FOSSILIZED TANIUS** (A CRESTLESS DINOSAUR) BUT BELONGED TO SOME OTHER PREHISTORIC **ANIMAL.**

●   **TRIASSIC**   ●   **JURASSIC**   ●   **CRETACEOUS**

NO MATTER WHICH THEORY IS RIGHT, **TSINTAOSAURUS** (OR **TANIUS**) BELONGED TO THE **HADROSAUR FAMILY**.

HADROSAURS EVOLVED AT THE **END** OF THE **CRETACEOUS PERIOD** AND WERE A VERY **DIVERSE** AND **POPULOUS GROUP**. THEIR PROPENSITY FOR **EATING** A WIDE VARIETY OF **PLANTS** ALLOWED THEM TO **SPREAD** AND **SURVIVE** IN MANY DIFFERENT **HABITATS** AND **CLIMATES**.

SCALE

IF THE **HORN** REALLY WAS ON TSINTAOSAURUS' **HEAD**, THEN IT WAS USED TO EMIT **SOUNDS**. SCIENTISTS SUPPORTING THIS **THEORY** THINK THAT SOME **SKIN** ON TOP OF THE HORN COULD HAVE BEEN **INFLATED** FOR THIS **PURPOSE**.

```
LENGTH:  30 FEET
HEIGH:   12 FEET
WEIGHT:   3 TONS
```

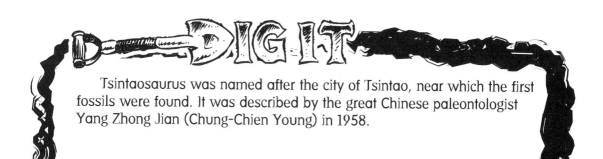

DIG IT

Tsintaosaurus was named after the city of Tsintao, near which the first fossils were found. It was described by the great Chinese paleontologist Yang Zhong Jian (Chung-Chien Young) in 1958.

PSITTACOSAURUS

sit-a-ko-sawr-us   *"Parrot Lizard"*

THIS **DINOSAUR'S NAME** COMES FROM THE GREEK WORD **"PSITTAKO,"** WHICH MEANS **"PARROT."** IT WAS CHOSEN BECAUSE **PSITTACOSAURUS'** STRONG BEAK RESEMBLES THAT OF A **PARROT.**

TRIASSIC   JURASSIC   CRETACEOUS

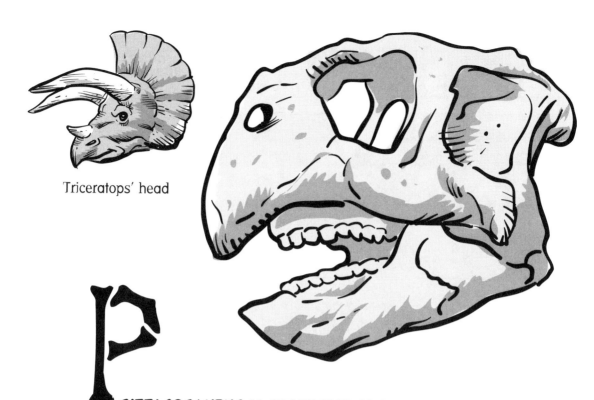

Triceratops' head

P SITTACOSAURUS IS CONSIDERED TO BE THE **ANCESTOR** OF THE **CERATOPSIAN DINOSAURS**, A GROUP INCLUDING **TRICERATOPS**. PSITTACOSAURUS AND TRICERATOPS SEEM **VERY DIFFERENT** FROM EACH OTHER. THE **FIRST** WAS A **BIPED**, HAD ONLY **FOUR FINGERS**, AND WAS **MISSING** TRICERATOPS' **BIG FRILL** AND **FACIAL HORNS**.

BUT THESE TWO DINOSAURS HAD VERY **SIMILAR FEATURES**. PSITTACOSAURUS' **THICKENED NOSE** AND **POINTY CHEEK BONES** EVOLVED INTO TRICERATOPS' **FACIAL HORNS**. BOTH HAD A **TRIANGULAR TOOTHLESS BEAK**, **CHEEK TEETH**, AND **JAW MUSCLES** ATTACHED TO A **BONE** AT THE **BACK** OF THEIR **HEADS**. IN **TRICERATOPS**, THIS BONE HAD **DEVELOPED** INTO A **BIG FRILL**. IN **PSITTACOSAURUS** IT WAS ONLY A **SMALL RIDGE**.

LENGTH: 8 FEET
HEIGHT: 4 FEET
WEIGHT: 100 LBS

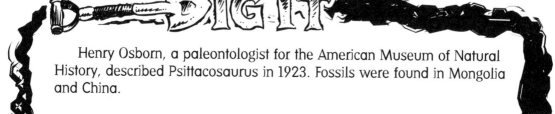

DIG IT

Henry Osborn, a paleontologist for the American Museum of Natural History, described Psittacosaurus in 1923. Fossils were found in Mongolia and China.

EORAPTOR

ee-oh-rap-tor   *"Dawn Thief"*

EORAPTOR WAS ONE OF THE **OLDEST DINOSAURS** EVER FOUND. THE MEANING OF ITS NAME, **"DAWN THIEF,"** REFERS TO WHEN THIS DINOSAUR **LIVED**, AT THE **DAWN** OF THE **AGE** OF **DINOSAURS**, **228 MILLION YEARS AGO!**

DIG IT

Eoraptor was found by paleontologist Ricardo Martinez in Argentina in 1991, during an expedition funded by the United States and Argentina. Eoraptor was named by Paul Sereno, Catherine Forster, Raymond Rogers, and Alfredo Monetta, who were all part of the expedition team.

EORAPTOR WAS A **SWIFT HUNTER** THAT CHASED **SMALL REPTILES.** ITS **TAIL** WAS KEPT **STRAIGHT** AND **STIFF,** AND HELPED EORAPTOR TO MAKE **QUICK TURNS** WHILE **RUNNING.**

LENGTH: 3 FEET
WEIGHT: 20 LBS

 Footnote: Eoraptor and Herrerasaurus were discovered in the same place in Argentina, during the same expedition. Both dinosaurs lived approximately at the same time and were carnivorous.

SCALE

TRIASSIC ● JURASSIC ● CRETACEOUS

EUOPLOCEPHALUS

you-oh-plo-sef-a-lus   *"Well Armored Head"*

EUOPLOCEPHALUS HAD **BONY PLATES** ALL OVER THE **UPPER PART** OF ITS **BODY**. THESE PLATES WERE **FUSED** TO ITS **BONES**, CREATING A **HARD SHELL**. IT MUST HAVE BEEN ALMOST **IMPOSSIBLE** FOR EUOPLOCEPHALUS' **ENEMIES** TO PENETRATE ITS **ARMOR**.

THIS **TANK-LIKE ANIMAL** ALSO HAD SPIKES ALL OVER ITS BODY, FROM ITS **HEAD** RIGHT DOWN TO ITS **TAIL**. EVEN ITS **NECK**, USUALLY A VERY **VULNERABLE PART**, WAS **WELL PROTECTED** WITH **SPIKES** AND **PLATES**.

● TRIASSIC ● JURASSIC ● CRETACEOUS

ITS EYELIDS WERE ALSO **PROTECTED!** **EUOPLOCEPHALUS** WAS ABLE TO **LOWER** A SET OF **BONY PLATES** OVER ITS **EYES** WHEN NEEDED.

EUOPLOCEPHALUS DEALT WITH ITS ATTACKERS BY **SWINGING** ITS **TAIL**, WHICH ENDED IN A **CLUSTER** OF **BONES.** EUOPLOCEPHALUS USED IT AS A **MALLET** TO **STRIKE** AND **SMASH** ITS **ENEMY'S BONES!**

EUOPLOCEPHALUS' ONLY **WEAKNESS** WAS ITS **BELLY. THIS** PART OF ITS BODY **WASN'T COVERED** WITH PLATES.

HOWEVER, **T. REX** OR OTHER **PREDATORS** WOULD HAVE HAD TO TURN EUOPLOCEPHALUS **UPSIDE DOWN** FIRST!

BUT WHEN ATTACKED, EUOPLOCEPHALUS WOULD **SQUAT,** MAKING IT **IMPOSSIBLE** FOR ITS PREDATOR TO REACH ITS **BELLY.** EUOPLOCEPHALUS NEEDED ONLY TO **WAIT** FOR ITS PREDATOR TO GET **WEARY** AND **LEAVE.**

EUOPLOCEPHALUS' **NAME** IS MADE UP OF **THREE GREEK WORDS** WHICH MEAN **"WELL ARMORED HEAD."** THEY REFER TO THE **PLATES** PROTECTING ITS **SKULL.**

LENGTH: 20 FEET
WEIGHT: 2 TONS

Euoplocephalus was named by Canadian paleontologist Lawrence Lambe in 1910.

TYRANNOSAURUS YUKs!

19. WHICH **DINOSAUR** WAS **COOLER** THAN **ALL OTHER DINOSAURS?**

—**HIP**-SILOPHODON!

20. WHAT DO YOU **CALL** A **DINOSAUR** THAT DOESN'T **TASTE** VERY **SWEET?**

—A DINO-**SOUR!**

21. WHAT KIND OF **TOOL** WOULD A **T. REX** USE IF IT WERE A **CARPENTER?**

—A DINO-**SAW-R!**

22. WHICH **DINOSAUR** IS **VERY CUTE** AND **COVERED** IN **WOOL?**

—**LAMB**-EOSAURUS!

23. WHAT DO **YOU** CALL A **DINOSAUR MAGICIAN?**

—A **WIZARD LIZARD!**

24. WHO ARE **ALBERTOSAURUS' FRIENDS?**

—**JAMES**-OSAURUS, **TIM**-OSAURUS, AND **WILLIAM**-OSAURUS!

APATOSAURUS

ah-pat-uh-sawr-us "Deceptive Lizard"

APATOSAURUS' HEAD WAS ONLY **TWO FEET LONG**. ITS **NECK**, ON THE OTHER HAND, WAS ABOUT **30 FEET LONG!**

DESPITE ITS **ENORMOUS WEIGHT**—UP TO **30 TONS** (THAT'S LIKE **800** 10-YEAR-OLD KIDS!), ITS **BRAIN** WAS ONLY AS BIG AS AN **APPLE!** IT WASN'T EVEN **BIG ENOUGH** TO **COORDINATE** THE WHOLE OF APATOSAURS' **BODY**. IN FACT, APATOSAURUS HAD TO RELY ON ITS **GANGLIA**, A **NERVE CENTER** LOCATED ON ITS **BACK**, TO CONTROL ITS **BACK LEGS** AND **TAIL MOVEMENTS!**

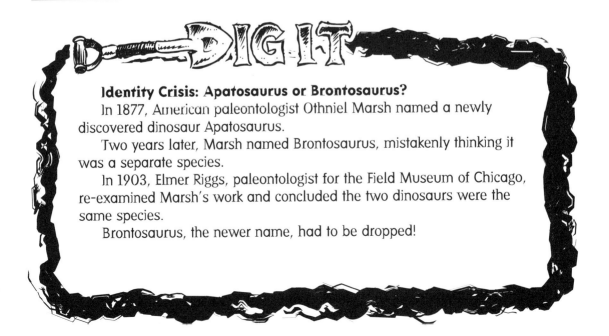

DIG IT

Identity Crisis: Apatosaurus or Brontosaurus?

In 1877, American paleontologist Othniel Marsh named a newly discovered dinosaur Apatosaurus.

Two years later, Marsh named Brontosaurus, mistakenly thinking it was a separate species.

In 1903, Elmer Riggs, paleontologist for the Field Museum of Chicago, re-examined Marsh's work and concluded the two dinosaurs were the same species.

Brontosaurus, the newer name, had to be dropped!

BRONTOSAURUS, APATOSAURUS' **OLD NAME,** MEANS **"THUNDER LIZARD"** BECAUSE IT WAS THOUGHT THAT, WHEN IT **WALKED,** THIS GIGANTIC DINOSAUR MUST HAVE MADE A **THUNDEROUS NOISE** DUE TO ITS **IMMENSE WEIGHT.**

APATOSAURUS' TEETH WERE VERY **SHARP** AND COULD RIP **PLANTS** AND **FOLIAGE,** BUT THEY COULD NOT **CHEW!** APATOSAURUS SWALLOWED SMALL **STONES,** CALLED **GASTROLITHS.** THEY MOVED AROUND IN ITS **GIZZARD** AND **GROUND DOWN** THE **FOOD.**

TRIASSIC   JURASSIC   CRETACEOUS

APATOSAURUS

SOME SCIENTISTS THINK **APATOSAURUS** USED ITS **NECK** TO REACH THE **TOP** OF THE **TREES** IN THE SAME WAY **GIRAFFES** DO TODAY.

LENGTH: 90 FEET
HEIGHT: 15 FEET

SCALE

Apatosaurus fossils have been found in Colorado, Oklahoma, Utah, and Wyoming.

NOT EVERYONE BELIEVES **APATOSAURUS** USED ITS **LONG NECK** TO REACH AND EAT **HIGH VEGETATION.**

J. MICHAEL PARRISH, A PALEONTOLOGIST, AND **KENT STEVENS,** A COMPUTER SCIENCE PROFESSOR, MEASURED **APATOSAURUS' FOSSILS** AND BUILT A **VIRTUAL REPLICA.**

BASED ON THEIR **RESEARCH,** THEIR **THEORY** IS THAT **APATOSAURUS** COULD NOT **RAISE** ITS **HEAD** ABOVE ITS **SHOULDERS!**

J. **MICHAEL PARRISH** AND **KENT STEVENS** THINK **APATOSAURUS** USED ITS **NECK** TO FEED OFF **PLANTS** GROWING IN **SWAMPY AREAS.** IT COULD REACH **VEGETATION** FAR AWAY WITHOUT GETTING ITS **FEET** STUCK IN **MUD.** FOR SUCH A **MASSIVE** AND **LUMBERING ANIMAL** BEING STUCK IN **MUD** MUST HAVE BEEN A **SCARY—OR EVEN DEADLY—SITUATION!**

Many animals that are now extinct lived at the same time as dinosaurs. Here are some of the weirder-looking ones!

ICHTHYOSAURUS

eek-thy-oh-sawr-us   "Fish Lizard"

ICHTHYOSAURUS LIVED IN THE SEA DURING THE **JURASSIC** AND **EARLY CRETACEOUS PERIODS.**

ICHTHYOSAURUS COULD BE MORE THAN **SIX FEET LONG** AND RESEMBLED A **MODERN DOLPHIN.** BUT DOLPHINS ARE **MAMMALS,** WHILE ICHTHYOSAURUS WAS A **REPTILE.**

THE **FIRST FOSSILS** OF ICHTHYOSAURUS WERE FOUND IN **LYME REGIS,** ENGLAND, IN 1809. THE DISCOVERERS WERE A **10-YEAR-OLD GIRL** NAMED **MARY ANNING** AND HER BROTHER **JOSEPH.**

SINCE 1809 A **MULTITUDE** OF ICHTHYOSAURUS' **FOSSILS** HAVE BEEN **FOUND,** MANY IN A **VERY GOOD STATE** OF PRESERVATION.
SEVERAL FOSSILS SEEM TO INDICATE THAT ICHTHYOSAURUS **GAVE BIRTH** TO ITS **YOUNG.**
IF THIS WAS TRUE, IT WOULD BE AN **EXTREMELY UNCOMMON FEATURE,** AS REPTILES GENERALLY **LAY EGGS.**

IN THE **PROCESS** OF **FOSSILIZATION,** SOFT TISSUES ARE GENERALLY **LOST FOREVER.** THE RARE DISCOVERY OF SOME ICHTHYOSAURUS **SKIN CELLS,** HOWEVER, SHOWED THIS ANIMAL HAD A **RED** AND **BROWN SKIN COLOR.**

ICHTHYOSAURUS IS ONE OF THE **BEST KNOWN** REPTILES DUE TO THE **NUMBER** OF **FOSSILS** RETREIVED AND THEIR **GOOD STATE** OF PRESERVATION.
IN ADDITION TO **SKELETONS, COPROLITES** (FOSSILIZED **POOP**) AND FOSSILIZED **STOMACH CONTENTS** WERE ALSO FOUND.
THESE ITEMS GIVE US AN IDEA OF ICHTHYOSAURUS' **DIET,** WHICH INCLUDED **FISH, MOLLUSKS,** AND **SQUID.**

Many animals that are now extinct lived at the same time as dinosaurs. Here are some of the weirder-looking ones!

PLESIOSAURS

Plae-syo-saurus   "Near Lizard"

Elasmosaurus, like all the long-necked Plesiosaurs, fed on small fish and crustaceans.

PLESIOSAURS WERE A **GROUP** OF **MARINE REPTILES** THAT LIVED THROUGHOUT THE **AGE OF THE DINOSAURS.**

PLESIOSAURS DESCENDED FROM A **COMMON ANCESTOR** AND **SPLIT** INTO **TWO MAIN GROUPS,** ONE WITH **SMALL HEADS** AND **LONG NECKS,** THE OTHER WITH **BIG SKULLS** AND **SHORT NECKS.**

ALL PLESIOSAURS **BREATHED AIR** AND HAD TO COME TO THE **SURFACE** EVERY ONCE IN A WHILE. THEY **LAID** THEIR **EGGS** ON **LAND,** WHERE THEY MOVED **CLUMSILY.**

BUT IN THE **SEA,** PLESIOSAURS COULD **TURN ON THE SPOT** TO GRAB SOME UNAWARE PREY, OR **GLIDE GRACEFULLY** THROUGH THE WATER BY **FLAPPING** ITS **POWERFUL FINS.**

ELASMOSAURUS' NECK (ON THE PREVIOUS PAGE) WAS **45 FEET LONG**, MORE THAN THE REST OF THIS REPTILE'S **BODY** AND **TAIL!** ITS **NECK** WAS MADE UP OF MORE THAN **70 VERTEBRAE**, THE MOST THAT ANY ANIMAL EVER HAD.

Plesiosaurus and all the Plesiosaurs had belly ribs.

PLESIOSAURUS LIVED DURING THE **EARLY JURASSIC PERIOD**. IT WAS **EIGHT FEET LONG** AND HAD **SHARP, CONIC TEETH**.

THE FIRST **FOSSILS** OF PLESIOSAURUS WERE FOUND BY **MARY ANNING**, THE 10-YEAR-OLD GIRL WHO ALSO DISCOVERED THE **FIRST FOSSILS** OF ICHTHYOSAURUS.

Kronosaurus fed on large fish.

KRONOSAURUS' SKULL WAS **NINE FEET LONG**, A **THIRD** OF ITS **BODY LENGTH**. WITH SUCH A HEAD, KRONOSAURUS COULD EAT **BIG FISH** AND **MARINE REPTILES**.

MUTTABURRASAURUS

mut-ah-burr-ah-sawr-us "Lizard from Muttaburra"

THE FIRST **MUTTABURRASAURUS** WAS FOUND IN **1963** BY **DOUG LANGDON.** DOUG WAS A **FARMER** IN **MUTTABURRA,** AUSTRALIA. ONE DAY, WHILE CROSSING THE **THOMPSON RIVER,** HE NOTICED A **WEIRD STONE.** IT TURNED OUT TO BE A FOSSIL OF A BRAND NEW **DINOSAUR.** THE SPECIMEN WAS CALLED **MUTTABURRASAURUS LANGDONI,** IN HONOR OF DOUG.

TRIASSIC ● JURASSIC ● CRETACEOUS

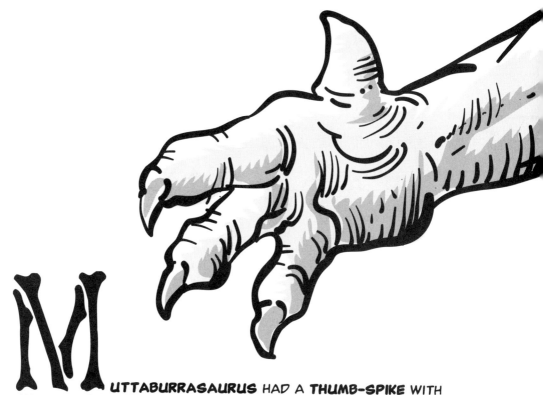

MUTTABURRASAURUS HAD A **THUMB-SPIKE** WITH WHICH IT **DEFENDED** ITSELF AGAINST **PREDATORS.** MUTTABURRASAURUS PROBABLY ALSO USED ITS THUMB-SPIKE TO UNEARTH **ROOTS** OR TO **FIGHT** OTHER **MEMBERS** OF ITS **HERD** DURING MATING SEASON.

VERY LITTLE IS KNOWN OF **DINOSAURS** THAT LIVED IN **AUSTRALIA,** AS VERY **FEW FOSSILS** HAVE BEEN FOUND. BUT SINCE THE **EIGHTIES,** A DOZEN SPECIES, INCLUDING **MUTTABURRASAURUS,** HAVE BEEN **UNEARTHED** AND **STUDIED.**

LENGTH: 23 FEET
HEIGH: 8 FEET

DIG IT

Muttaburrasaurus was described by Australian paleontologists Alan Bartholomai and Ralph Molnar in 1981.

DASPLETOSAURUS

das-plee-toe-sawr-us   *"Frightful Lizard"*

PALEONTOLOGISTS THINK **DASPLETOSAURUS** DIDN'T GIVE **CHASE** TO ITS **PREY** BECAUSE IT WAS **TOO BULKY** AND COULDN'T **RUN** FOR **VERY LONG.**

DASPLETOSAURUS MIGHT HAVE **HUNTED** BY **HIDING** BEHIND **SHRUBS,** AND **ATTACKED** ITS **UNAWARE VICTIMS.**

BY **BITING** WITH ITS **SAW-LIKE TEETH,** IT MADE **ESCAPE** IMPOSSIBLE FOR ITS **PREY.**

DASPLETOSAURUS TORE OFF **CHUNKS** OF **MEAT** WITH ITS **HUGE MOUTH,** AND **SWALLOWED** THEM WITHOUT **CHEWING.**

TRIASSIC ● JURASSIC ● CRETACEOUS

D ASPLETOSAURUS WAS A LITTLE OVER HALF THE **SIZE** OF **T. REX.** IT MIGHT HAVE BEEN **T. REX'S ANCESTOR,** BUT AS ONLY A **FEW DASPLETOSAURUS FOSSILS** HAVE BEEN FOUND SO FAR, THIS **THEORY** HAS NOT BEEN **CONFIRMED.**

DIG IT

In 1921, fossil hunter Charles Sternberg discovered the first fossils of Daspletosaurus. He thought they belonged to Gorgosaurus. This species had already been described and named by Lawrence Lambe in 1914.

In 1970, Dale Russell, Senior Curator of Paleontology for the North Carolina Museum of Natural Science, studied the fossils again. He concluded Gorgosaurus and the fossils Sternberg had found were two different species. He called the new species Daspletosaurus.

UNSOLVED MYSTERIES

"PLESIOSAURUS"

Although extinct for millions of years, prehistoric animals
seem to reappear in the most unlikely places!

IN 1977, A **JAPANESE TRAWLER**
FISHED OUT OF THE **PACIFIC OCEAN**
A **CREATURE** WITH A SMALL **HEAD,**
LONG **NECK,** AND **FINS.**

IT APPEARED TO BE A
PLESIOSAURUS. BUT PLESIOSAURUS
BECAME EXTINCT **65 MILLION YEARS
AGO,** WHILE THIS **ANIMAL** HAD
DIED ONLY A **FEW DAYS** BEFORE
BEING CAUGHT!

ONE THING WAS FOR **SURE:**
WHATEVER IT WAS, IT WAS
DECOMPOSING.

THE **CAPTAIN** OF THE TRAWLER
ALLOWED THE **FISHERMEN** TO TAKE
SOME **PHOTOS** AND **FLESH
SAMPLES.**

THEN THE **CARCASS** HAD TO BE
THROWN BACK INTO THE OCEAN: IT
SMELLED AWFUL!

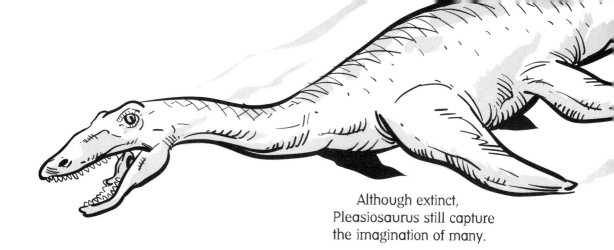

Although extinct,
Pleasiosaurus still capture
the imagination of many.

THE **NEWS** WENT AROUND THE **GLOBE,** BUT SOME PEOPLE WEREN'T SURPRISED. THEY CLAIMED THE **CARCASS** WAS MERELY A **BASKING SHARK.**

THE JAW OF THIS KIND OF SHARKS OFTEN **FALLS OFF** AFTER THEY **DIE** AND START **DECOMPOSING.** THE JAW-LESS ANIMAL LOOKS EERILY LIKE A **PLESIOSAURUS.**

STILL OTHER PEOPLE DECLARED THAT **PLESIOSAURUS** AREN'T **EXTINCT** AFTER ALL! THEY SPECULATED THAT A **PLESIOSAURUS** HAD BEEN **FROZEN** IN THE **SOUTH POLE.** THEN, AN **ICEBERG** CONTAINING THE ANIMAL EVENTUALLY **BROKE OFF** AND **FLOATED** TO THE **SOUTH PACIFIC.** PLESIOSAURUS GOT **FREED** FROM THE MELTING **ICE,** BUT **DIED** AND **ROT** BEFORE GETTING **FISHED OUT** BY THE TRAWLER.

WHAT DO **YOU** THINK ABOUT THIS **MYSTERY** OF THE **DEEP?**

Basking sharks are very
peaceful animals that feed
on plankton.

STRUTHIOMIMUS

strooth-ee-oh-my-mus "Ostrich-Like"

STRUTHIOMIMUS WAS BORN TO **RUN!** IT HAD VERY **LONG FEET,** AND ITS **SHINS** WERE **LONGER** THAN ITS **THIGHS—** A **FEATURE** TYPICAL OF **FAST-MOVING DINOSAURS.**

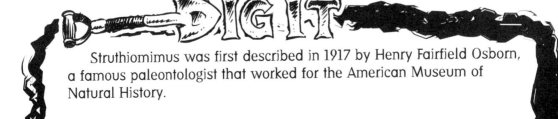

DIG IT

Struthiomimus was first described in 1917 by Henry Fairfield Osborn, a famous paleontologist that worked for the American Museum of Natural History.

STRUTHIOMIMUS WAS SO SIMILAR TO A **MODERN OSTRICH** THAT IT WAS NAMED "OSTRICH-LIKE."

STRUTHIOMIMUS DISPLAYED MANY **CHARACTERISTICS** TYPICAL OF **MODERN OSTRICHES,** SUCH AS **POSTURE, SKELETON,** LARGE **EYES,** AND **BEAK.**

WHILE **OSTRICHES** HAVE **WINGS** AND CAN **RUN** UP TO **50** MILES PER HOUR, **STRUTHIOMIMUS** HAD **GRASPING HANDS** AND COULD ONLY RUN UP TO **30** MILES PER HOUR. BUT IT WAS STILL ONE OF THE **FASTEST** MOVING **DINOSAURS!**

LENGTH: 20 FEET
HEIGHT: 5 FEET
WEIGHT: 700 LBS

Struthiomimus was omnivorous—it ate both vegetation and other animals. It probably fed on fruits, insects, plants, and small reptiles like lizards.

SCALE

TRIASSIC   JURASSIC   CRETACEOUS

AVIMIMUS

ah-vee-mee-mus "Bird-Like"

THE FIRST FOSSILS OF **AVIMIMUS** BAFFLED SCIENTISTS. THEY THOUGHT IT WASN'T A **DINOSAUR** AT ALL, BUT A **BIRD ANCESTOR.** SOME THOUGHT IT WAS A **CHIMAERA.** PALEONTOLOGISTS CALL A BEWILDERING **MIX** OF **FOSSILS** OF **TWO** OR MORE **ANIMALS** A CHIMAERA. IN THIS CASE, THE TWO ANIMALS WERE THOUGHT TO BE AN **ANCIENT BIRD** AND A **DINOSAUR.**

WHEN ADDITIONAL FOSSILS WERE FOUND, IT WAS CLEAR THAT **AVIMIMUS** WAS A **DINOSAUR** AFTER ALL, EVEN IF IT SHOWED MANY **BIRD CHARACTERISTICS.**

TRIASSIC ● JURASSIC ● CRETACEOUS

SOME **GROOVES** FOUND ON ITS **ARMS** INDICATED **AVIMIMUS** HAD **FEATHERS.** ITS **BRAINCASE** WAS **LARGER** AND ITS **EYE SOCKETS ROUNDER** THAN OTHER **DINOSAURS.** ALL **THREE** OF THESE **FEATURES** ARE TYPICAL IN **BIRDS.**

ON THE OTHER HAND, THE **GROOVES** ON AVIMIMUS' ARMS MIGHT HAVE **JUST** BEEN A SIGN OF A **TIME-WORN FOSSIL.** ALSO, AVIMIMUS' **HIP BONE** SHOWED IT WAS A **SAURISCHIAN DINOSAUR** AND NOT A BIRD.

 Footnote: Avimimus was insectivorous.

L E N G T H :   5   F E E T
W E I G H T :   3 0   L B S

Avimimus was named by Russian paleontologist Sergei Mikhailovich Kurzanov in 1981.

DIPLODOCUS

di-plod-oh-kuss   *"Double Beam"*

IN 1901, **ANDREW CARNEGIE**, A **STEEL MAGNATE** ENAMORED OF **DINOSAURS**, DECLARED HE WANTED TO FIND A DINOSAUR **"AS BIG AS A BARN."** HE FINANCED AN **EXPEDITION** TO THE **MORRISON FORMATION** IN THE **WESTERN UNITED STATES.**

WITHIN THE MANY **FINDINGS**, A **COMPLETE SKELETON** OF **DIPLODOCUS** WAS UNEARTHED AND NAMED **DIPLODOCUS CARNEGIE** IN ANDREW'S HONOR.

Diplodocus' name means "Double Beam" and refers to this dinosaur's double row of bones in its spine.

DIPLODOCUS, LIKE OTHER **SAUROPODS** SUCH AS **BRACHIOSAURUS** AND **APATOSAURUS,** HAD A VERY LONG NECK. IT COULD BE UP TO **25 FEET LONG!** DIPLODOCUS ALSO HAD A 45-FOOT-LONG WHIP-LIKE TAIL.

BUT DIPLODOCUS' HEAD WAS **VERY SHORT**—LESS THAN **TWO FEET LONG!**

DIPLODOCUS' TEETH COULDN'T **CHEW!** IN ORDER TO **DIGEST** THE **VEGETATION** IT ATE, **DIPLODOCUS** SWALLOWED **SMALL STONES** CALLED **GASTROLITHS.** THE **GASTROLITHS** MOVED AROUND IN ITS **GIZZARD** AND **GROUND DOWN** THE **FOOD.**

LENGTH: 80 FEET
WEIGHT: 15 TONS

 TRIASSIC JURASSIC CRETACEOUS

IGUANODON

eeh-gwa-no-don **"Iguana Tooth"**

IGUANODON HAD **FIVE FINGERS** ON EACH HAND. THE **THUMB** WAS A **BIG SPIKE-CLAW,** PROBABLY USED FOR **STABBING** ITS **PREDATORS.**
THREE OF ITS **FIVE FINGERS** WERE **HOOFED,** BECAUSE **IGUANODON** WALKED ON ITS **BACK FEET,** BUT SOMETIMES WENT DOWN ON **ALL FOUR.**
IGUANODON'S **LAST FINGER** WASN'T HOOFED, BUT WAS **FLEXIBLE** AND COULD HAVE BEEN USED, ALONG WITH THE OTHERS, TO **GRAB FOOD.**

SCALE

TRIASSIC   JURASSIC   CRETACEOUS

X-RAY VISUALIZATION

Look at this page while holding it up to a window to see Iguanodon's skeleton!

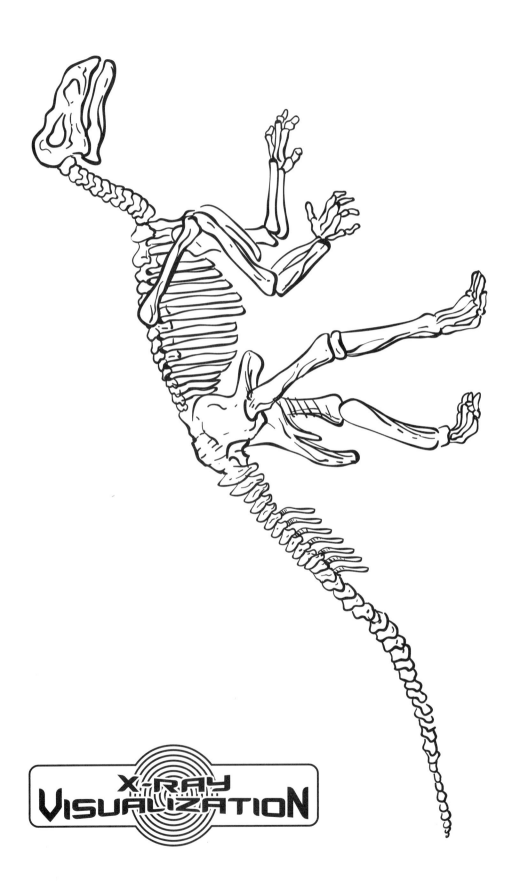

X-RAY VISUALIZATION

FOSSILIZED FOOTPRINTS and BONE BEDS, where a
lot of animals died together, suggest that
Iguanodon lived in herds.

LENGTH: 30 FEET
WEIGHT: 6 TONS

IGUANODON WAS THE **SECOND DINOSAUR** EVER TO BE
RECOGNIZED AS AN **EXTINCT ANIMAL** AND RECEIVE A **SCIENTIFIC
NAME** (THE FIRST WAS **MEGALOSAURUS**). ENGLISH PHYSICIAN
GIDEON MANTELL THOUGHT IT WAS A **HUGE REPTILE,** ALTHOUGH
SCIENTISTS AT THE TIME BELIEVED IT TO BE A MERE **RHINOCEROS.**
THIS WAS **BEFORE** THE TERM **"DINOSAUR"** WAS EVEN INVENTED!

IGUANODON'S FOSSILS HAVE BEEN DISCOVERED AROUND THE **WORLD.**
UNLIKE MOST HERBIVORES, **IGUANODON** WAS ABLE TO EAT MANY DIFFERENT
KINDS OF **PLANTS,** THRIVING IN A **VARIETY** OF **HABITATS.**

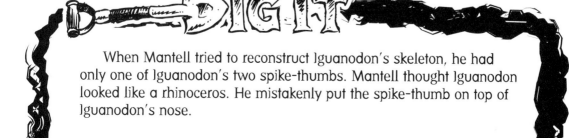

DIG IT

When Mantell tried to reconstruct Iguanodon's skeleton, he had
only one of Iguanodon's two spike-thumbs. Mantell thought Iguanodon
looked like a rhinoceros. He mistakenly put the spike-thumb on top of
Iguanodon's nose.

MEGALOSAURUS

mega-lo-sawr-us   *"Great Lizard"*

MEGALOSAURUS WAS A
FIERCE CARNIVORE. IT HAD
SERRATED TEETH, CLAWED
HANDS AND FEET, AND A
HUGE HEAD.

SCALE

● TRIASSIC ● JURASSIC ● CRETACEOUS

IN 1677, A **MYSTERIOUS FOSSIL** WAS DISCOVERED BY **ROBERT PLOT,** KEEPER OF THE **ASHMOLEAN MUSEUM** IN OXFORD, ENGLAND. HE THOUGHT IT BELONGED TO A **GIANT.**

THE **MYSTERY** REMAINED **UNSOLVED** UNTIL **1824,** WHEN **WILLIAM BUCKLAND,** AN ENGLISH SCIENTIST, ACQUIRED SOME **FOSSILS** DISCOVERED NEAR **OXFORD.** HE CONCLUDED THESE **FOSSILS** AND THE ONE DESCRIBED BY **PLOT** BELONGED TO AN **UNKNOWN LIZARD.** HE NAMED IT **"MEGALOSAURUS."** BUT IT WAS ONLY IN **1842** THAT **SIR RICHARD OWEN** INTRODUCED THE **IDEA** THAT **MEGALOSAURUS** WAS AN **EXTINCT REPTILE,** BELONGING TO A **GROUP** HE CALLED **"DINOSAURS."**

WILLIAM BUCKLAND THOUGHT **MEGALOSAURUS** WAS **70 FEET LONG!** MEGALOSAURUS WAS A **VERY BIG DINOSAUR,** BUT IT ONLY MEASURED **30 FEET IN LENGTH.**

DIG IT

Megalosaurus' bones and fossilized trackways were found in England and France.

Many animals that are now extinct lived at the same time as dinosaurs. Here are some of the weirder-looking ones!

METRIORHYNCHUS

met-rio-reen-kus   "Moderate Snout"

METRIORHYNCHUS WAS A **CROCODILE** THAT HAD **EVOLVED** TO **SURVIVE** IN **WATER.** UNLIKE **LAND-DWELLING CROCODILES** THAT HAVE VERY **COARSE** AND **SCALY SKIN,** METRIORHYNCHUS' **SKIN** WAS **SMOOTH** AND **LIGHTWEIGHT.** IN THIS WAY, METRIORHYNCHUS COULD **GLIDE** IN THE **WATER** WITHOUT **RESISTANCE.**

METRIORHYNCHUS WAS A **REPTILE** THAT LIVED DURING THE **LATE JURASSIC PERIOD.** TWO OF ITS CONTEMPORARIES WERE **CETIOSAURUS** AND **COMPSOGNATHUS.**

METRIORHYNCHUS' **FOSSILS** HAVE BEEN FOUND IN **ENGLAND, FRANCE, AND CHILE.**

TO **PROPEL** ITSELF THROUGH **WATER,** METRIORHYNCHUS USED ITS **FINS** AND **FISH TAIL.** METRIORHYNCHUS WAS A **PISCIVORE.** HE COULD **CAPTURE** ITS **PREY** WITH HIS **NEEDLE-LIKE TEETH.**

PROTOCERATOPS

proh-to-ser-ah-tops   *"First Horned Face"*

PROTOCERATOPS WAS AN **ANCESTOR** OF THE **HORNED DINOSAURS**. IT DIDN'T REALLY HAVE A **HORN** ON ITS **FACE**, ONLY A **BUMP**, WHICH WAS **USED** LIKE A HORN.

PROTOCERATOPS HAD A **BULKY BODY** AND **SHORT LEGS**. IT PROBABLY DIDN'T **RUN** VERY **FAST**, SO IT HAD TO RELY ON ITS **BEAK** AND **FRILL** FOR **PROTECTION**.

TRIASSIC   JURASSIC   CRETACEOUS

OME PALEONTOLOGISTS THINK **PROTOCERATOPS MALES** HAD **BIGGER FRILLS** AND **NOSE BUMPS** THAN **FEMALES**. THIS WAS BECAUSE MALES **FOUGHT** EACH OTHER DURING MATING SEASON FOR **LEADERSHIP** WITHIN THE **HERD**.

LENGTH: 9 FEET
HEIGHT: 3 FEET
WEIGHT: 1 TON

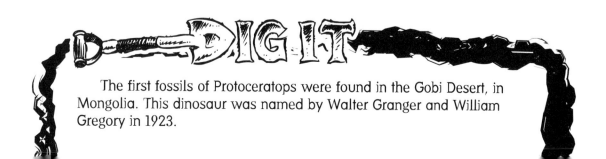

DIG IT

The first fossils of Protoceratops were found in the Gobi Desert, in Mongolia. This dinosaur was named by Walter Granger and William Gregory in 1923.

HADROSAURUS

had-row-sawr-us   *"Bulky Lizard"*

HADROSAURUS BELONGED TO THE **DUCK-BILLED GROUP** OF **DINOSAURS**. THE BEAK WAS **TOOTHLESS**, BUT BEHIND IT, THESE DINOSAURS HAD A **MULTITUDE** OF **SELF-REPLACING TEETH**.

BOTH **BEAK** AND **TEETH** ALLOWED **HADROSAURUS** TO EAT A **LARGE VARIETY** OF **VEGETATION**, EVEN **VERY TOUGH-TO-CHEW KINDS**.

TRIASSIC   **JURASSIC**   **CRETACEOUS**

LENGTH: 30 FEET
WEIGHT: 4 TONS

Hadrosaurus' wrong "kangaroo" stance.

THE FIRST FOSSILIZED **HADROSAURUS** SKELETON WAS FOUND IN **1858** BY **WILLIAM PARKER FOULKE** IN **HADDONFIELD**, NEW JERSEY. HE SHIPPED THE **DISCOVERY** TO SCIENTIST **JOSEPH LEIDY**, WHO NAMED IT.

HADROSAURUS WAS THE **FIRST DINOSAUR** TO BE **DESCRIBED** IN THE **UNITED STATES.**

FOULKE'S DISCOVERY WAS MISSING ITS **SKULL,** BUT IT WAS OTHERWISE IN A VERY GOOD SHAPE. SCIENTISTS WERE ABLE TO **LEARN** FROM IT THAT SOME DINOSAURS WERE BIPEDAL.

IN 1868, **BENJAMIN WATERHOUSE HAWKINS,** WHO HAD PREVIOUSLY BUILT A **REPLICA** OF **IGUANODON** FOR **SIR RICHARD OWEN,** MOUNTED **HADROSAURUS' SKELETON** FOR THE **FIRST TIME** ON A **TWO-FEET STANCE.** UNFORTUNATELY, HADROSAURUS WAS THOUGHT TO BE A **KANGAROO-LIKE** ANIMAL, SO IN ITS **POSE** IT RESTED ON ITS **TWO FEET** AND **TAIL.**

Hadrosaurus' correct stance.

SCIENTISTS NOW KNOW THAT HADROSAURUS' "KANGAROO" STANCE WAS **WRONG.**

HADROSAURUS USED ITS **TAIL** TO BALANCE ITS **HEAD,** MORE LIKE A **CHICKEN.**

Footnote: Hadrosaurus was semi-bipedal. It could stand and walk on its two back feet, but preferred to run on four.

NOT SO CUTE, AFTERALL!

In 1994, 14-year-old dinosaur hunter **Wes Linster** found a **fossilized dinosaur skull**. He named it **Bambi** because it was **small**. Wes thought it might have belonged to a **cute** and **cuddly dinosaur**, just like Disney's famous **deer**.

Bambi turned out to be a **brand new dinosaur**. The studies concluded that when Bambi was alive, it wasn't **cute** and **cuddly** at all. Despite its **small size**, Bambi was a **fierce predator** that lived **72** million years ago. It was extremely **intelligent**, had **feathers** and several other **bird features**.

Some paleontologists think Bambi is another **missing link** between **dinosaurs** and **birds**. But some scientists argue that when Bambi **lived**, birds had already **evolved**.

This dinosaur's final **scientific name** is **Bambiraptor**. It was named in **1999** by several paleontologists, including **Dave Burnham, Kriag Derstler,** and **John Ostrom**.

DINOSAUR DOODY!

COPROLITE IS THE **SCIENTIFIC NAME** FOR **FOSSILIZED POOP.** IT WAS COINED IN 1829 BY **REVEREND WILLIAM BUCKLAND,** (WHO NAMED **MEGALOSAURUS**). AT THE TIME, BUCKLAND WAS STUDING SOME FOSSILIZED **SHARK DROPPINGS** HE FOUND IN LYME REGIS, ENGLAND.

COPROLITES CONTAIN **FOSSILIZED REMAINS** OF WHAT THE **DINOSAUR** HAD FOR **SUPPER. HERBIVORES' DUNG** CONTAINS **SEEDS, LEAVES, STEMS,** OR **CONIFER NEEDLES. CARNIVORES' DUNG** CONTAINS THEIR **PREY'S CRUSHED BONES** AND **TEETH.** BUT IT'S VERY **HARD** FOR SCIENTISTS TO FIGURE OUT EXACTLY WHICH **DINOSAUR** DID IT!

In case you were wondering, coprolites don't smell!

PERHAPS THE MOST **FAMOUS COPROLITE** UNEARTHED SO FAR IS ONE FOUND IN **CANADA** IN 1996. AN **EXPEDITION** ORGANIZED BY THE **ROYAL SASKATCHEWAN MUSEUM** WAS EXCAVATING SOME **T. REX FOSSILS.** AT SOME **DISTANCE** FROM THE **SITE,** PALEONTOLOGISTS FOUND A **CURIOUSLY-SHAPED ROCK.**

SCIENTIST **KAREN CHIN** CONCLUDED THAT IT WAS A **65-MILLION-YEARS-OLD POOP.** IT CONTAINED **FRAGMENTS** OF **BONES** OF A **DINOSAUR,** PROBABLY A **BABY TRICERATOPS.** THE **COPROLITE** WAS MORE THAN **ONE FOOT LONG** AND, BECAUSE OF ITS **CONTENT** AND **SIZE,** IT WAS PROBABLY DROPPED BY A **T. REX.**

TARBOSAURUS

tar-bo-sawr-us   *"Alarming Lizard"*

TARBOSAURUS WAS VERY SIMILAR TO **T. REX**. BOTH HAD PUNY **ARMS**, A HUGE **HEAD**, AND A SET OF **SHARP TEETH**. BUT **TARBOSAURUS** WASN'T QUITE AS **BIG** AS **T. REX**.

SCALE

TRIASSIC   JURASSIC   CRETACEOUS

TARBOSAURUS' **FEET** HAD **FOUR TOES. THREE** SUPPORTED TARBOSAURUS' **WEIGHT.** THE **FOURTH ONE** WAS A **DEWCLAW** AND DID NOT REACH THE **GROUND.**

TARBOSAURUS HAD ONLY **TWO FINGERS** ON ITS **HANDS.**

TARBOSAURUS WAS A **FIERCE CARNIVORE.** IT PROCURED FOOD BY **HUNTING** OR BY **STEALING** THE **PREY** OTHER **MEAT-EATING DINOSAURS** CAUGHT.

LENGTH: 46 FEET
WEIGHT: 5 TONS

Tarbosaurus was named in 1955 by Russian paleontologist Evgenii Aleksandrovich Maleev.

DINOSAUR Q&A

Brachiosaurus is the biggest dinosaur of which the most complete skeleton has been unearthed.

Brachiosaurus was 80 feet long and weighted 70 tons.

But Argentinosaurus was probably the biggest of them all. Unfortunately, only a few massive bones were discovered.

Jose Bonaparte and Rodolfo Coria were the two Argentinian paleontologists who first found Argentinosaurus. They estimate it was 120 feet long and weighed 90 tons!

WHICH WAS THE **BIGGEST MEAT-EATING DINOSAUR?**

Long thought to be T. rex, a recent discovery found Giganotosaurus to be the biggest so far.

Giganotosaurus was about 45 feet long and weighed up to 8 tons.

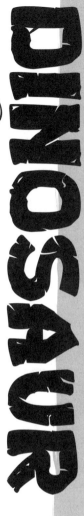

WHICH WAS THE SMALLEST DINOSAUR?

The smallest dinosaur ever found was Micropachycephalosaurus (my-kro-pak-ee-sef-ah-lo-sore-us), a 20-inch-long dinosaur.

Ironically, this little guy has the longest name of all the dinosaurs! Its 23-letter name means "small, thick-headed lizard."

WHICH IS THE SHORTEST DINOSAUR NAME?

It's Minmi, a 10-foot-long armored dinosaur.

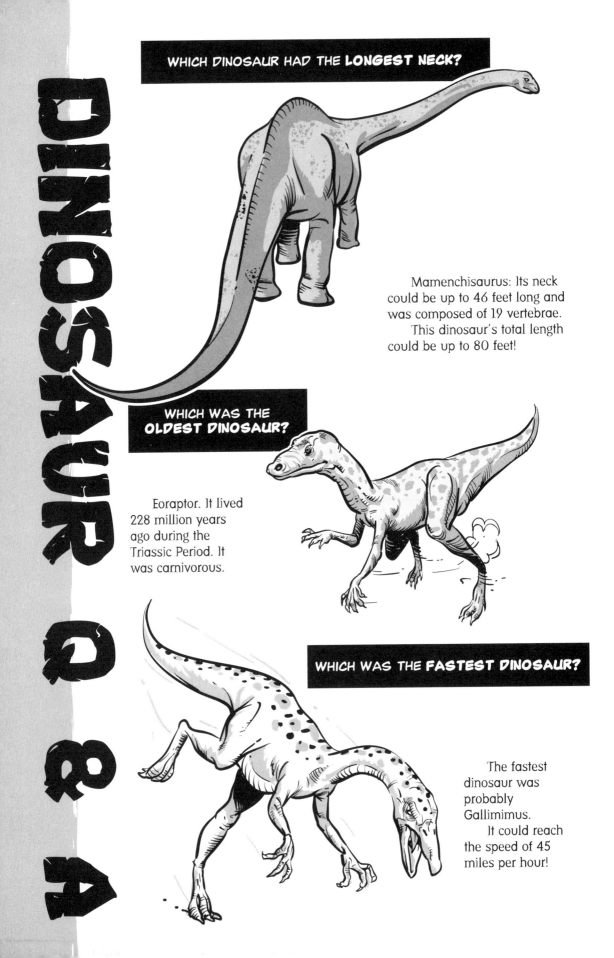

DINOSAUR Q & A

WHICH DINOSAUR HAD THE LONGEST NECK?

Mamenchisaurus: Its neck could be up to 46 feet long and was composed of 19 vertebrae. This dinosaur's total length could be up to 80 feet!

WHICH WAS THE OLDEST DINOSAUR?

Eoraptor. It lived 228 million years ago during the Triassic Period. It was carnivorous.

WHICH WAS THE FASTEST DINOSAUR?

The fastest dinosaur was probably Gallimimus. It could reach the speed of 45 miles per hour!

WHICH WAS THE SMARTEST DINOSAUR?

Intelligence is measured by comparing the weight of an animal's brain to the weight of its body.

Troodon seems to have been the smartest of all dinosaurs, with a big brain for its body size.

Troodon also had big, round eyes, and might have been able to see and hunt at night.

WHICH WAS THE DUMBEST DINOSAUR?

It might have been Stegosaurus: its brain was the size of a walnut!

Stegosaurus' brain wasn't even big enough to control body movements. This dinosaur had to rely on its ganglia, a nerve center situated near its spine.

The ganglia helped to coordinate the movements of Stegosaurus' back legs.

Stegosaurus' ganglia was bigger than its brain!

DINOSAUR Q & A

PACHYCEPHALOSAURUS

pack-eeh-sef-al-oh-sawr-us "Thick-Headed Lizard"

SCALE

PACHYCEPHALOSAURUS' SKULL COULD BE UP TO **TEN INCHES THICK**, AND PROBABLY GREW **THICKER** WITH **AGE**.

TRIASSIC   JURASSIC   CRETACEOUS

SOME SCIENTISTS THINK **PACHYCEPHALOSAURUS MALES** USED TO **RAM** AGAINST EACH OTHER DURING **MATING FIGHTS**.

BUT **MARK GOODWIN** FROM THE UNIVERSITY OF CALIFORNIA AT BERKELEY SAYS THAT DESPITE ITS **THICKNESS,** PACHYCEPHALOSAURUS' **SKULL** WAS **FRAGILE.** IF PACHYCEPHALOSAURUS MALES **RAMMED** THEIR **HEADS** AGAINST EACH OTHER, THEY WOULD HAVE CAUSED EACH OTHER **BAD INJURIES** OR EVEN **DEATH.** SO THE REASON THIS DINOSAUR HAD SUCH A **THICK SKULL** IS STILL A **MYSTERY!**

L E N G T H :   1 5   F E E T
W E I G H T :   9 5 0   L B S

ONLY A **FEW SKULLS** OF **PACHYCEPHALOSAURUS** HAVE BEEN FOUND SO FAR, SO THIS DINOSAUR'S **HEIGHT** AND **WEIGHT** CAN ONLY BE **ESTIMATED.**

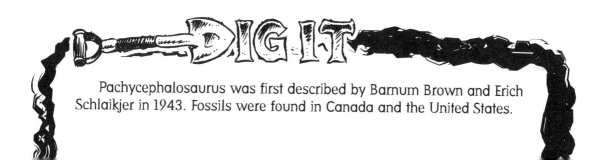

Pachycephalosaurus was first described by Barnum Brown and Erich Schlaikjer in 1943. Fossils were found in Canada and the United States.

BAGACERATOPS

bah-gah-ser-uh-tops   *"Small-Horned Face"*

BAGACERATOPS BELONGS TO THE **PROTOCERATOPSIDAE** FAMILY. THEY WERE THE **ANCESTORS** OF THE **CERATOPSIANS**, THE **HORNED DINOSAURS**.

BAGACERATOPS HAD MANY **TRAITS** TYPICAL OF THE **CERATOPSIANS**, BUT IN **SMALLER VERSIONS**. FOR EXAMPLE, ITS **SIZE**, AS WELL AS ITS **FRILL** (THE BONY **PROTECTION** AROUND ITS **NECK**), WERE MUCH **SMALLER** COMPARED TO ITS **DESCENDANTS**.

SCALE

TRIASSIC   JURASSIC   CRETACEOUS

ITS **TURTLE-LIKE BEAK** HAD NO **TEETH,** BUT WAS VERY **SHARP** AND ABLE TO **CRUSH** TOUGH **VEGETATION** AND **ROOTS.**

BAGACERATOPS LAID **EGGS,** CARED FOR ITS **LITTLE ONES,** AND TRAVELED IN **HERDS.**

Footnote: This dinosaur's name means "small-horned face" because the horn on its nose was small compared to those of other horned dinosaurs.

DIG IT

Bagaceratops was discovered in 1975 in Mongolia, by paleontologists Teresa Maryanska and Halszka Osmolska.

TROODON

troh-don   *"Wounding Tooth"*

TROODON WAS ONE OF THE **SMARTEST DINOSAURS.** **INTELLIGENCE** IS MEASURED BY COMPARING AN **ANIMAL'S BRAIN SIZE** TO ITS **BODY SIZE.** IF A **VERY LARGE ANIMAL** HAS A **SMALL BRAIN,** IT'S NOT VERY INTELLIGENT. TROODON'S **BRAIN** WAS **VERY BIG** FOR ITS **BODY SIZE.**

TRIASSIC   JURASSIC   CRETACEOUS

ROODON WASN'T ONLY **VERY SMART. ITS EYES** WERE **VERY LARGE** AND **FACING FORWARD,** GIVING **TROODON** A GOOD **SENSE** OF **DEPTH** AND **NIGHT VISION.** TROODON WENT HUNTING IN **PACKS** AT **DUSK.**

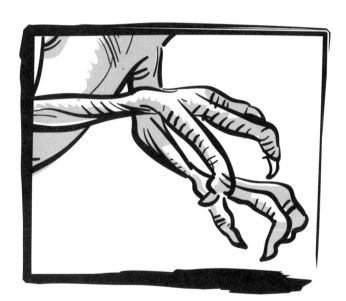

ROODON'S HANDS WERE VERY GOOD FOR **GRASPING,** AND EACH OF ITS **THREE FINGERS** HAD A POWERFUL **CLAW** AT THE END OF IT.

DIG IT

In 1854, American explorer Ferdinand Vandiveer Hayden found some teeth in the Judith River, in Montana. They were the first dinosaur remains ever to be found in North America.

The teeth were shipped to scientist Joseph Leidy, who studied them and decided they belonged to several dinosaurs, one of which he named Troodon in 1856.

Nothing more was known of Troodon until the 1980s, when some fossilized bones were finally unearthed.

TROODON

LIKE **VELOCIRAPTOR**, TROODON HAD A **BIG CLAW** ON ITS **FOOT**.

VELOCIRAPTOR COULD HUNT **DINOSAURS** MUCH **BIGGER** THAN ITSELF, WHILE **TROODON** PROBABLY HUNTED ONLY BABY **DINOSAURS**, **SMALL REPTILES**, OR **MAMMALS**.

WHEN **TROODON** LIVED, THERE WERE ONLY A **FEW MAMMALS** AND THEY WERE PROBABLY ONLY **SMALL NOCTURNAL RODENTS**. **DINOSAURS** WERE SO **WIDESPREAD** AND **VARIED** THAT **MAMMALS** COULD NOT **PROLIFERATE**.

Troodon's fossils have been found in Canada, Mexico, the United States, Tajikistan, and Uzbekistan (the last two countries are in Asia).

SOME **FOSSILS** OF **DINOSAURS** CLOSELY RELATED TO **TROODON** HAVE BEEN FOUND BEARING **FEATHER MARKS.** IT IS POSSIBLE, THEN, THAT **TROODON** ALSO HAD **FEATHERS.**

TROODON USED ITS **STIFF TAIL** TO BALANCE ITS **MOVEMENTS.** ITS **TAIL** HELPED **TROODON** TO MAKE **FAST TURNS** AND TO CHANGE **DIRECTION** WHILE CHASING PREY.

← SCALE →

HEIGHT: 9 FEET

WEIGHT: 100LBS.

◄ LENGTH: 12 FEET ►

WHY DID DINOSAURS BECOME EXTINCT?
THE K/T EVENT

DINOSAURS SEEM TO HAVE VANISHED **65 MILLION YEARS AGO,** LEAVING BEHIND ONLY **FOSSILS.** THIS **MASS EXTINCTION** IS CALLED THE **K/T EVENT.**

THE LETTER **"K"** STANDS FOR **"CRETA"** THE LATIN WORD FOR **CHALK,** FROM WHICH THE WORD **CRETACEOUS** COMES FROM. DURING THE **CRETACEOUS PERIOD,** A LAYER OF **CHALK** WAS DEPOSITED ON OUR PLANET. EVERYTHING **BURIED** UP TO THAT **LAYER** LIVED **65 MILLION YEARS AGO,** OR **MORE.**

THE LETTER **"T"** STANDS FOR **TERTIARY,** THE **PERIOD** OF THE **CENOZOIC ERA** STARTING AFTER THE **AGE OF DINOSAURS.** WE ARE STILL **LIVING** IN THE **CENOZOIC ERA** TODAY.

Triceratops was one of the last dinosaurs to become extinct. It probably saw what caused the dinosaurs extinction, 65 million years ago.

T. rex witnessed the K/T event and didn't survive. In fact, there are no fossils of T. rex to be found over the chalk layer of the Cretaceous Period.

SUDDEN AND DRAMATIC **CHANGES** IN THE **ENVIRONMENT** COULD HAVE CAUSED THE **DEMISE** OF **DINOSAURS.**

THE **K/T EVENT** WAS A **PHENOMENON** SO **CATASTROPHIC** ITS EFFECTS WERE FELT **AROUND THE GLOBE.** AFTER THE **K/T EVENT,** ALL **DINOSAURS, FLYING REPTILES,** AND **MARINE REPTILES,** EXCEPT TURTLES, WERE **WIPED OUT.** BUT WHAT **CAUSED** IT?

THE K/T EVENT

ONE **THEORY** STATES THAT AN **EXTRATERRESTRIAL OBJECT,** SUCH AS A **HUGE METEORITE,** HIT THE **EARTH** 65 MILLION YEARS AGO. THE IMPACT STARTED A DRAMATIC **CHAIN** OF **EVENTS** THAT BROUGHT TO THE **EXTINCTION** OF **DINOSAURS.**

THIS **THEORY** WAS PROPOSED IN **1980** BY TWO SCIENTISTS, **LOUIS ALVAREZ** AND HIS SON, **WALTER ALVAREZ.** AMAZINGLY, **TEN** YEARS LATER, THE **CRATER** SUPPOSEDLY LEFT BY THE IMPACT OF THE METEORITE WAS **ACCIDENTALLY DISCOVERED.** IT'S LOCATED UNDER THE **SEA,** NEAR THE **YUCATAN PENINSULA** IN MEXICO!

LOUIS AND WALTER ALVAREZ'S THEORY CLAIMS THAT, 65 MILLION YEARS AGO, A **SIX MILE WIDE ASTEROID**, TRAVELING AT THE SPEED OF **60 MILES** PER **HOUR**, HIT THE **EARTH** AND **EXPLODED** LIKE A **HUGE BOMB**. THE CRATER THAT WAS LEFT WAS **100 MILES WIDE** AND **4 MILES DEEP**.

THE **IMMEDIATE REACTIONS** TO SUCH AN **IMPACT** WERE **WAVES** AND **WILDFIRES**. THE **WAVES** WERE **HALF A MILE HIGH** AND **FLOODED** THE **COASTS** ALL AROUND THE **GULF OF MEXICO**. THEY **DROWNED** THE **ANIMALS** AND **DESTROYED** THE **VEGETATION**. THE **WILDFIRES** SPREAD ALL OVER THE **SURROUNDING LANDS**, BURNING **FORESTS** AND KILLING **ANIMALS**.

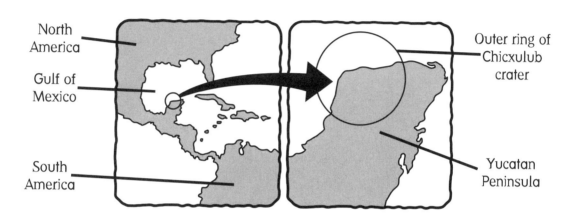

North America

Gulf of Mexico

South America

Outer ring of Chicxulub crater

Yucatan Peninsula

THE **ASTEROID EXPLOSION** CAUSED **DUST** TO GO UP INTO THE **ATMOSPHERE**. THE **DUST** WAS SO **THICK** THAT THE **SUN** WAS **OBSCURED** FOR **ONE WHOLE YEAR**. DURING THIS VERY **LONG NIGHT**, THE **TEMPERATURE** DROPPED AND **STORMS** PLAGUED THE **EARTH**. THE **EFFECTS** WERE FELT FOR A **LONG PERIOD** OF TIME, MAYBE EVEN **ONE MILLION YEARS**.

DINOSAURS SIMPLY COULDN'T **KEEP UP** WITH SO MANY **DRASTIC ENVIRONMENTAL CHANGES**. THEY DIED MOSTLY BECAUSE **FOOD** WAS **SCARCE** AND IT WAS **TOO COLD**.

SO, ACCORDING TO THIS **THEORY**, THIS IS HOW **DINOSAURS** AND **MANY REPTILES** BECAME **EXTINCT**.
ONE **QUESTION** REMAINS UNANSWERED: WHY DID **MAMMALS, BIRDS, FISH,** AND **INSECTS** SURVIVE THE **K/T EVENT?**

THE K/T EVENT

SCIENTISTS DISCOVERED ANOTHER **65-MILLION-YEAR-OLD PHENOMENON.** DURING THE **CRETACEOUS PERIOD,** THERE WERE MANY MORE **ACTIVE VOLCANOS** THAN TODAY. ONE **REGION** WHERE **VOLCANOS** WERE ESPECIALLY **ACTIVE** WAS THE **DECCAN TRAPS,** LOCATED IN **INDIA.**

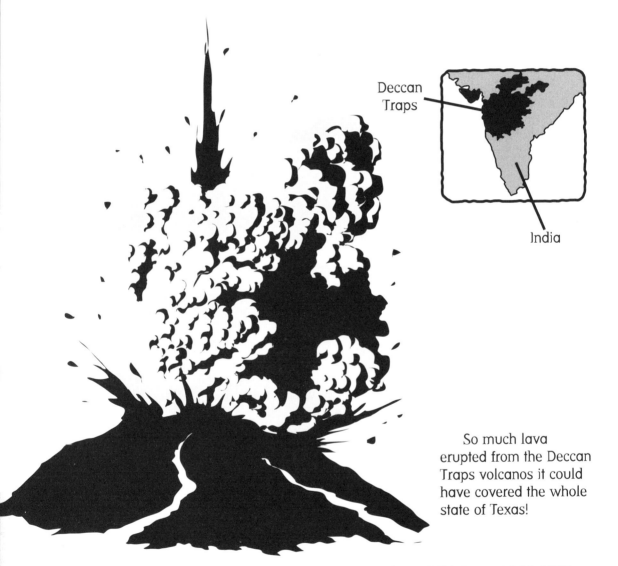

Deccan Traps

India

So much lava erupted from the Deccan Traps volcanos it could have covered the whole state of Texas!

SOME SCIENTISTS THINK SUCH **MASSIVE VOLCANIC ACTION** BROUGHT **SIDE EFFECTS** SIMILAR TO THOSE OF AN **ASTEROID IMPACT.** THE **SOOT** RELEASED DURING **VOLCANIC EXPLOSIONS** WAS **ENOUGH** TO **OBSCURE** THE **SUN** FOR A **PROLONGED TIME.** A **LONG COLD NIGHT** BROUGHT **FAMINE** AND **DEATH.**

IN ADDITION, SOME THINK **VOLCANIC ACTIVITY** PRODUCED A HIGH **QUANTITY** OF **CARBON DIOXIDE.** THIS **GAS** IS THE **CAUSE** OF THE **"GREENHOUSE EFFECT."**
BY **ACCUMULATING** IN THE **ATMOSPHERE,** CARBON DIOXIDE MADE THE **TEMPERATURE** RISE. IN TURN, THE **HOT WEATHER** CAUSED **DESTRUCTIVE STORMS** AND **DESERTIFICATION.**

BUT EVEN THIS **THEORY** DOESN'T **EXPLAIN** WHY THE **K/T EVENT** WAS SO SELECTIVE, KILLING SOME SPECIES AND LEAVING OTHERS **UNTOUCHED.**

WHY DID DINOSAURS BECOME EXTINCT?
THE K/T EVENT

THE **K/T** WAS SUCH A **DRAMATIC EVENT** THAT IS BOUND TO BE INTERPRETED BY **MANY THEORIES.** HERE ARE SOME OF THE MORE **INTERESTING ONES...**

THEORY #1

THE **SUN** HAS A **TWIN,** CALLED **NEMESIS.** THE SUN AND NEMESIS **ORBIT** AROUND **EACH OTHER.**

WHEN NEMESIS COMES **NEAR ENOUGH** TO OUR SUN, ITS **GRAVITY** SENDS **COMETS** AND **ASTEROIDS** OUT OF THEIR **ORBITS.**

SOME OF THEM **CRASH** INTO **EARTH,** STARTING A DESTRUCTIVE **CHAIN** OF **EVENTS.**

Nemesis and the Sun meet every 25 to 30 million years and that's why we have never seen them together.

THEORY #2

FLOWERING PLANTS EVOLVED DURING THE CRETACEOUS PERIOD, WHEN THE DINOSAURS BECAME EXTINCT. FLOWERING PLANTS WERE **POISONOUS** FOR **HERBIVOROUS DINOSAURS.** ONCE **ALL** THESE **HERBIVORES** DIED, **CARNIVOROUS DINOSAURS** DIDN'T HAVE ANYTHING TO EAT, AND **DIED** OF **STARVATION.**

THEORY #3

R.I.P.

JUST LIKE A **SINGLE INDIVIDUAL** IS BORN, LIVES, AND, AFTER A CERTAIN AMOUNT OF TIME, **DIES,** SO DO **GROUPS** OF **ANIMALS.**

THIS THEORY CLAIMS THAT **DINOSAURS** SIMPLY **AGED** AND **DIED** AS A **GROUP.**

THEORY #4

ONE **THEORY** SUGGESTS THAT A **METEORITE** CARRYING **HARMFUL VIRUSES** HIT THE EARTH. THE VIRUSES INFECTED THE **DINOSAURS,** MAKING THEM **SICK** AND EVENTUALLY **KILLING** THEM ALL.

THE VIRUSES WEREN'T HARMFUL TO THE **SPECIES** THAT **SURVIVED** THE K/T EVENT, LIKE **FISH** AND **MAMMALS.**

THEORY #5

SCIENTISTS NOTICED THAT TOWARD THE **END** OF THE **CRETACEOUS PERIOD,** MANY **DINOSAURS** HAD ALREADY BECOME **EXTINCT.** A **SMALL METEORITE** IMPACT WOULD HAVE EASILY **KILLED** THE **FEW** REMAINING ONES.

UNTIL WE LEARN **MORE** ABOUT WHAT **HAPPENED** AT THE **END** OF THE **CRETACEOUS PERIOD,** ALL THESE **THEORIES** ARE **SPECULATION**...MAYBE **DINOSAURS** WERE **ABDUCTED** BY ALIENS AND NOW **LIVE HAPPILY** ON A **PLANET** FAR, FAR **AWAY!**

The Dinosaurs' Legacy
BIRDS

THE **EXTINCTION** OF **DINOSAURS** 65 MILLION YEARS AGO LEFT A **VOID** THAT WAS FILLED BY THE **MAMMALS.** BUT THE **DINOSAURS' LEGACY** LIVED ON IN ANOTHER GROUP, THE **BIRDS.**

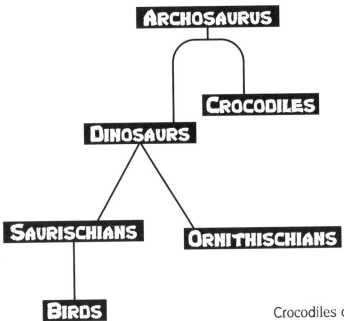

Crocodiles and Dinosaurs had a common reptilian ancestor, Archosaurus.

Birds evolved from the Saurischian dinosaurs.

THE **IDEA** THAT **BIRDS** DESCEND FROM **DINOSAURS** WAS FIRST PROPOSED IN 1869 BY ZOOLOGIST **THOMAS HUXLEY. OTHNIEL MARSH** WAS ALSO A **PROMOTER** OF THIS **CONTROVERSIAL THEORY.**

THESE **TWO SCIENTISTS** THOUGHT THE **SIMILARITIES** BETWEEN **ARCHAEOPTERYX,** A BIRD ANCESTOR, AND **COMPSOGNATHUS,** A DINOSAUR, WERE **COMPELLING EVIDENCE:** AT ONE TIME, A **GROUP** OF **DINOSAURS** EVOLVED INTO **BIRDS,** AND TOOK **FLIGHT.**

ALTHOUGH **ARCHAEOPTERYX** WAS A **BIRD ANCESTOR,** IT COULD STILL BE CALLED A **DINOSAUR.**

BUT THE **SCIENTIFIC COMMUNITY** OF THE TIME THOUGHT THE IDEA PREPOSTEROUS AND PUT IT TO **REST.**

EVENTUALLY, THE **THEORY** THAT **BIRDS DESCEND** FROM **DINOSAURS** RESURFACED. TODAY IT IS **WIDELY ACCEPTED** THAT **BIRDS** AND **DINOSAURS** ARE CLOSELY **RELATED.** THEY ARE MORE CLOSELY RELATED THAN **DINOSAURS** ARE TO **REPTILES.**

SO, THE NEXT TIME YOU HEAR A **BIRD CHIRPING** OR SEE IT **FLYING AROUND,** REMEMBER THAT THERE'S A LOT MORE **T. REX** IN IT THAN IN ANY OTHER **ANIMAL** NOW LIVING ON **EARTH!**

GLOSSARY

BONE BED
A LOCATION WHERE SEVERAL ANIMALS DIED AND WERE BURIED TOGETHER.

BIPED, BIPEDAL
BIPEDS ARE ANIMALS THAT WALK ON TWO FEET. VELOCIRAPTOR WAS BIPEDAL.

CANNIBALISM
THE PRACTICE OF AN ANIMAL EATING ITS OWN KIND. FOR EXAMPLE, COELOPHYSIS ATE ITS OWN YOUNG.

CARNOSAUR
A GROUP OF CARNIVOROUS AND BIPEDAL DINOSAURS WITH CLAWED HANDS. EUSTREPTOSPONDYLUS AND MEGALOSAURUS WERE BOTH CARNOSAURS.

CARNIVORE, CARNIVOROUS
A MEAT-EATING ANIMAL. ALBERTOSAURUS WAS CARNIVOROUS.

CHEEK TEETH
THE TEETH THAT ARE UP AGAINST THE CHEEKS.

CHIMAERA
AN IMPOSSIBLE ANIMAL MADE OF A BEWILDERING MIX OF FOSSILS OF TWO OR MORE ANIMALS.

CONIFER
A KIND OF EVERGREEN THAT PRODUCES CONE-SHAPED FRUITS. A PINE TREE IS A CONIFER.

CYCADS
CYCADS ARE PALM-LIKE TREES THAT EVOLVED DURING THE PALEOZOIC ERA, 300 MILLION YEARS AGO, AND STILL EXIST TODAY.

DEWCLAW
A FOOT CLAW THAT DOES NOT REACH THE GROUND.

DINOSAUR
A LAND-DWELLING REPTILE THAT IS NOW EXTINCT.

FERN
A PLANT THAT DOESN'T BEAR FLOWERS AND REPRODUCES ITSELF BY RELEASING SPORES.

FRILL
A RUFFLE OF BONE AND SKIN, OFTEN ADORNED WITH SPIKES, FOUND AROUND THE NECK OF THE HORNED DINOSAURS.

GANGLION
A NERVE CENTER LOCATED OUTSIDE THE BRAIN.

GASTRALIA
A SET OF RIBS NOT ATTACHED TO THE SPINE AND EMBEDDED IN THE SKIN SURROUNDING THE BELLY. GASTRALIA PROTECT DELICATE INTERNAL ORGANS, LIKE THE STOMACH AND INTESTINES. MANY DINOSAURS AND REPTILES, LIKE T. REX AND PLESIOSAURUS, HAD GASTRALIA.

GASTROLITHS
SMALL STONES FOUND IN THE GIZZARD OF SOME ANIMALS. THEY ARE SMOOTH AND HELP THE ANIMAL GRIND DOWN THE FOOD BEFORE IT GETS INTO THE STOMACH.

GIZZARD
A SACK SITUATED BEFORE THE STOMACH OF SOME ANIMALS LIKE APATOSAURUS OR MODERN CHICKENS. THE GIZZARD CONTAINS GASTROLITHS.

HERBIVORE, HERBIVOROUS
A PLANT-EATING ANIMAL. MAIASAURA WAS HERBIVOROUS.

HERPETOLOGIST
A SCIENTIST THAT STUDIES REPTILES.

HORSETAIL
A KIND OF FLOWERLESS PLANT WITH HOLLOW STEMS.

ICHTHYOLOGIST
A SCIENTIST THAT STUDIES FISH.

INSECTIVORE, INSECTIVOROUS
AN ANIMAL THAT EATS INSECTS. A MOLE IS INSECTIVOROUS.

MAMMAL
WARM-BLOODED ANIMALS, INCLUDING HUMANS, THAT HAVE THEIR SKIN COVERED WITH HAIR. MAMMALS HAVE MAMMARY GLANDS THAT PRODUCE MILK FOR THEIR YOUNG. REPTILES AND DINOSAURS ARE NOT MAMMALS.

MORRISON FORMATION
A REGION IN THE WEST OF THE UNITED STATES AND CANADA THAT EXTENDS FOR ABOUT ONE MILLION SQUARE MILES. IT INCLUDES SEVERAL STATES FROM NEW MEXICO TO MONTANA. IT WAS NAMED AFTER THE TOWN OF MORRISON, COLORADO, WHERE ARTHUR LAKES FOUND THE FIRST FOSSILS OF APATOSAURUS IN 1877. SINCE THEN SEVERAL DINOSAURS HAVE BEEN UNEARTHED IN THE MORRISON FORMATION, INCLUDING ALLOSAURUS, STEGOSAURUS, BRACHIOSAURUS, AND MANY MORE.

MYA
SHORT FOR MILLION YEARS AGO.

NICHE
THE LIFESTYLE OF AN ORGANISM AND ITS RELATIONSHIP TO ITS ENVIRONMENT.

NOCTURNAL
AN ANIMAL OR A PLANT THAT IS MORE ACTIVE DURING THE NIGHT THAN DURING THE DAY. AN OWL IS A NOCTURNAL BIRD OF PREY.

NODOSAURIDS
NAMED AFTER NODOSAURUS, THIS GROUP INCLUDED HERBIVOROUS DINOSAURS BEARING A PROTECTIVE KNOBBY SHIELD ON THEIR BACK. THEY EVOLVED IN THE JURASSIC PERIOD AND DIED OUT IN THE LATE CRETACEOUS PERIOD.

ORNITHISCHIAN (BIRD-HIPPED)
ONE OF THE TWO GROUPS IN WHICH DINOSAURS ARE DIVIDED. ORNITHISCHIANS WERE HERBIVOROUS DINOSAURS WITH A HIP BONE SIMILAR TO THAT OF MODERN BIRDS.

ORNITHOPODS (BIRD-FOOTED)
A GROUP OF ORNITHISCHIAN DINOSAURS. THEY HAD CHEEK POUCHES TO HOLD FOOD INSIDE THEIR MOUTH.

PISCIVORE, PISCIVOROUS
AN ANIMAL THAT PREDOMINANTLY EATS FISH. SPINOSAURUS WAS PISCIVOROUS.

PREHENSILE
THE ABILITY TO GRAB THINGS. FOR EXAMPLE, SOME MONKEYS HAVE A PREHENSILE TAIL, WHICH MEANS THEIR TAIL CAN GRASP THINGS LIKE TREE BRANCHES.

PTEROSAURS
A GROUP OF FLYING REPTILES THAT LIVED DURING THE LATE TRIASSIC PERIOD AND BECAME EXTINCT AT THE END OF THE CRETACEOUS PERIOD. PTERODACTYLUS AND EUDIMORPHODON WERE BOTH PTEROSAURS.

QUADRUPED, QUADRUPEDAL
AN ANIMAL WALKING ON FOUR FEET. A DOG IS QUADRUPEDAL.

REPTILE
AN ANIMAL WITH SCALY SKIN THAT REPRODUCES BY LAYING EGGS. MOST REPTILES ARE COLD-BLOODED. DINOSAURS, CROCODILES, AND SNAKES ARE ALL REPTILES.

SAURISCHIAN (LIZARD-HIPPED)

ONE OF THE TWO GROUPS IN WHICH DINOSAURS ARE DIVIDED. SAURISCHIANS WERE BOTH CARNIVOROUS AND HERBIVOROUS DINOSAURS WITH A HIP BONE SIMILAR TO THAT OF REPTILES.

SAUROPODS (LIZARD-FOOTED)

A GROUP OF DINOSAURS THAT EVOLVED IN THE TRIASSIC PERIOD AND BECAME EXTINCT AT THE END OF THE JURASSIC PERIOD. SAUROPODS WERE ALSO CALLED LONG-NECKED DINOSAURS. THEY WERE ALL QUADRUPEDALS AND HERBIVOROUS. SAUROPODS ARE THE ONLY HERBIVOROUS SAURISCHIANS. ALL THE OTHER SAURISCHIANS WERE CARNIVOROUS.

SCAVENGER

AN ANIMAL THAT EATS DEAD OR DYING ANIMALS. TURKEY VULTURES ARE SCAVENGERS.

SERRATED TEETH

TEETH WITH JAGGED EDGES LIKE A STEAK KNIFE.

STRIDE LENGTH

THE DISTANCE BETWEEN AN ANIMAL'S FEET WHILE WALKING. BY MEASURING THE STRIDE LENGTH OF FOSSILIZED FOOTPRINTS, PALEONTOLOGISTS CAN ESTIMATE THE SPEED THE DINOSAUR MOVED AT.

TYPE SPECIMEN

THE ORIGINAL SPECIMEN THAT GIVES THE NAME TO A WHOLE SPECIES AND AGAINST WHICH ALL THE OTHERS ARE COMPARED.